The role of special guardianship:

Best practice in permanency planning for children (England and Wales)

John Simmonds

BAAF
ADOPTION
& FOSTERING

Published by
British Association for Adoption & Fostering
(BAAF)
Saffron House
6-10 Kirby Street
London EC1N 8TS
www.baaf.org.uk

Charity registration 275689 (England and Wales) and SC039337
(Scotland)

British Library Cataloguing in Publication Data
A catalogue record for this book is available from the British Library
ISBN 978 1 907585 21 0

Project management by Jo Francis, BAAF
Designed and typeset by Helen Joubert Design
Printed in Great Britain by the Lavenham Press

BAAF is the leading UK-wide membership organisation for all those concerned with adoption, fostering and child care issues.

Contents

of the issues set out in their application in securing the long-term welfare and development of the child. Creating a stable and meaningful family life for any child where their birth parents cannot provide this is challenging and requires the co-operative effort of a large number of agencies and professionals. Where children cannot return home to parents or relatives, and where they cannot be adopted, foster care is the most likely placement for most children.

For children who are looked after, special guardianship was expected to be suitable where a child had developed a strong relationship and place in the foster carer's family and this had become evidenced over time. There was little likelihood of the child returning to their parent/s and no reason why the child should remain in care to the local authority. Evidence from Schofield (2002; 2003) and Biehal (2010) suggests that stable, planned and well supported long-term fostering has comparable outcomes to other forms of permanent placement, at least into adolescence. For some of these placements, the continuing supervisory role of the authority is questionable and may be unnecessary. This is a particular issue where a child has become a significant and meaningful part of the foster family but where the local authority holds and exercises parental responsibility and the carer does not and cannot.[2] Other issues of concern may involve the stigma and lack of "normality" for children in care. Special guardianship was planned to provide a solution to these kinds of situations. The making of the order by the court would legally establish the child as a member of the foster carer's family and enable the child to leave care while preserving a basic legal link with their birth parents and family. The statutory guidance identifies special guardianship as providing 'a firm foundation on which to build a lifelong permanent relationship between the child and their carer' (para. 5).

This scenario provides a picture of continuity from care proceedings, through to placement with approved carers, stability and belonging, with the local authority having a core role in bringing this about. Special guardianship might then be thought of as an obvious next step in normalising the life of the child and the carers, a legal step that was not previously available. The status of the order as a private law order is an understandable part of this continuity. Confining the process of making the order to an application by the prospective special guardians, the preparation of a report to court, and the assessment and provision of support seems proportionate. The other necessary work to safeguard the child and promote the child's welfare will have been achieved

2 There are efforts being made to ensure that some aspects of day-to-day decision making are delegated to foster carers (Loughton, 2010; http://www.education.gov.uk/inthenews/inthenews/a0064160/tim-loughton-calls-for-more-support-for-foster-carers; Fostering Network; http://www.fostering.net/delegated-authority)

through public law processes and through the local authority exercising its statutory responsibilities.

There are many other scenarios where special guardianship may be the right legal order to secure a permanent arrangement for the child. The conditions that give eligibility to apply for an order are wide ranging and the circumstances are not by any means confined to children who are in public care. The fact that an application can be made following the consent of specified parties or in the course of any family proceedings means that, in practice, an application may be made for special guardianship at the beginning or very near the beginning of the prospective special guardian's relationship with the child. It is even possible in some cases that an order might be made during the course of proceedings *without* an application having been made. Subject to a court report being made available in the prescribed form, the making of the order in these cases actually *begins* the relationship. There are other examples of local authorities taking a decision that the child should be placed for adoption, and a placement order application being made and a competing application being made for a special guardianship order – especially if family or friends came forward in the course of proceedings.

There is nothing in the flexibility of special guardianship to suggest that its status as a private law order lessens the importance of any applicant, child or child's parents fully understanding the significance of what is being applied for and the significant changes that the making of the order will bring about in the life of the child and the special guardian. As has been learnt with adoption and foster care, information, advice, preparation, training and support are critically important for all concerned. This guidance explores how this applies to special guardianship when these processes have not been explicitly identified and structured into the regulations and statutory guidance in the way that they are in adoption or foster care. The guidance also considers the role of social workers and local authorities in facilitating these processes. High quality practice, informed by expertise in family placement and child development, are as central to special guardianship as they are in adoption and foster care. In addition, as will be identified, there is also the additional factor of expertise in family and friends care. This is an unanticipated but very significant part of what research and practice experience tell us about the use to which the order has been applied.

Special guardianship offers a real opportunity for providing permanence for children who otherwise may not have achieved it. The lessons from the first period of implementation have raised some serious challenges, which are the focus of this guidance. Throughout, it is hoped that, whatever issues remain to be addressed, the focus on the immediate and long-term needs of the child and the special guardian/s are always at the forefront of thinking and practice.

2

What do we know about the use of special guardianship?

The national statistics to March 2010 in England indicate a quick take up of special guardianship orders in the first two years following implementation, followed by a slowing down in the last three years. The figures make a distinction between those orders made to former foster carers and others, although they do not in the former category make a distinction between family and friends carers and "stranger" foster carers.

These figures do not include those orders made where the child was not looked after. Currently it is difficult to identify how many children this might affect. The Judicial and Court statistics are calculated for a different period and on a different basis. In 2009, they show 890 orders made in public law proceedings and 720 in private law proceedings.

Children leaving care via a special guardianship or residence order

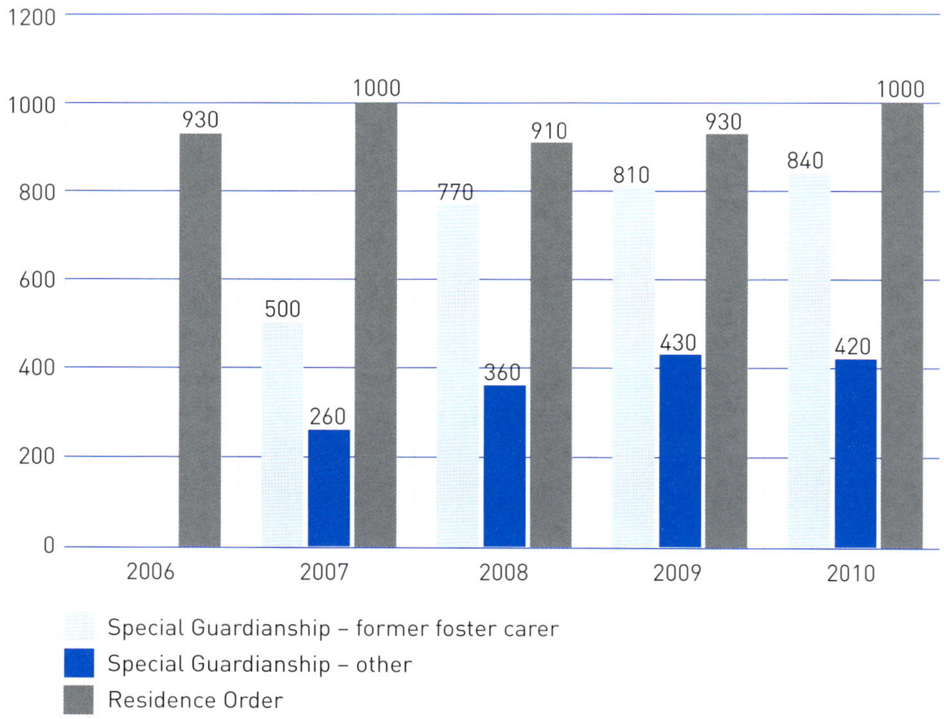

If these figures are broken down into numbers for each local government region, there is evidence of differences in take up. If the figures for each local authority are explored, there is also wide variation with many having no reported cases. It is difficult to be precise about an explanation for this, but local variation is commonly identified in many studies of the looked after children system.

England: Special guardianship orders – looked after children

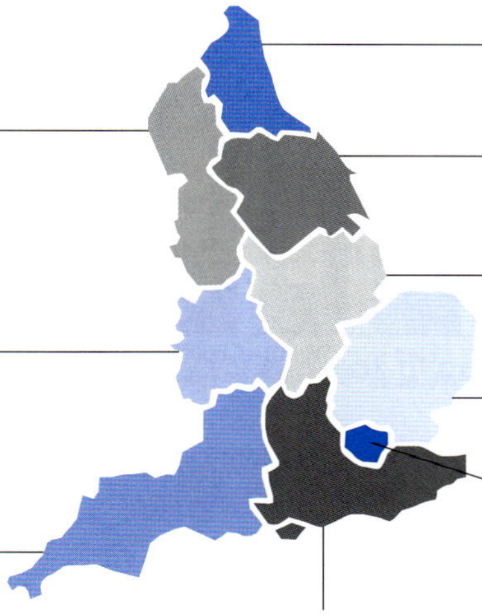

Source: Department for Education
First figure – Orders to 31.3.2007. Second figure – Orders to 31.3.2008.
Third figure – Orders to 31.3.2009 Fourth figure – Orders to 31.3.2010

The figures for Wales are much smaller, but that reflects the smaller numbers of children and carers to whom the order might be relevant. For the year ending 31 March 2010, 230 children ceased to be looked after through the making of an adoption order, 45 through a special guardianship order made to a former foster carer and 15 to a non-former foster carer.

The variations across English regions can also be seen if the percentages of children leaving care in any one year are calculated for the route that they took. Again, there is significant variation without a clear explanation of what exactly determines this.

The pathway to special guardianship

Type of carers (Hall, 2008)

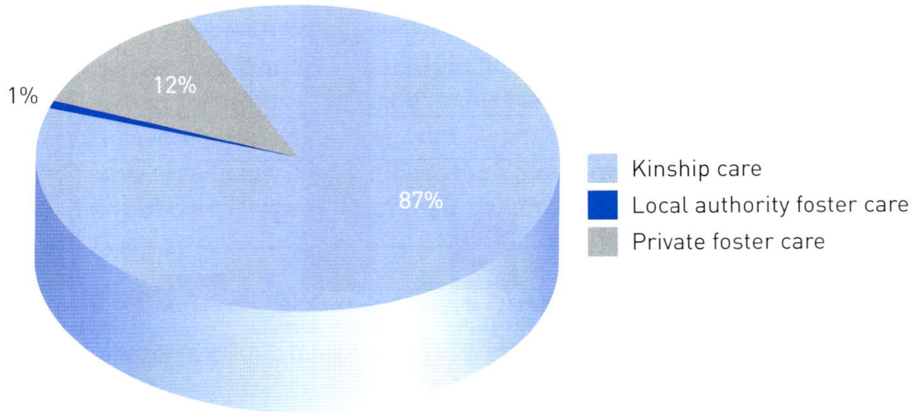

One of the most striking factors from these two studies and from practice experience is the extent to which special guardianship has become a solution for family and friends carers. In the Hall study (2008), family and friends carers amounted to 87 per cent, with 68 per cent of these being grandparents. In the Wade study, a similar profile was found.

Relationship of family and friends carer to the child

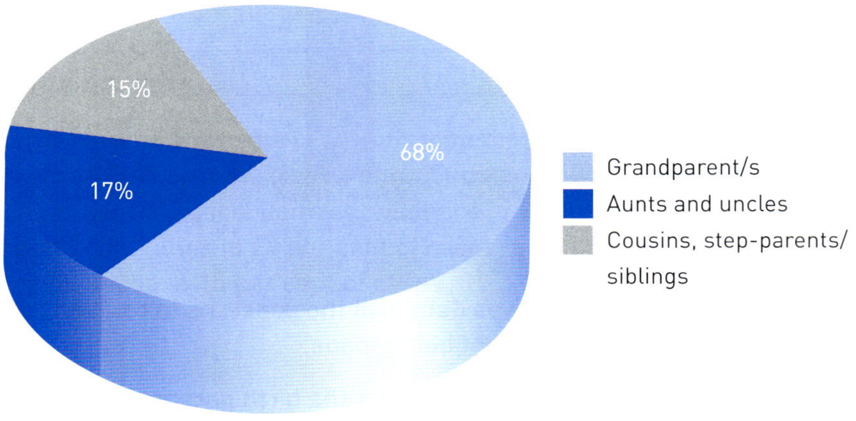

Child's relationship to carers

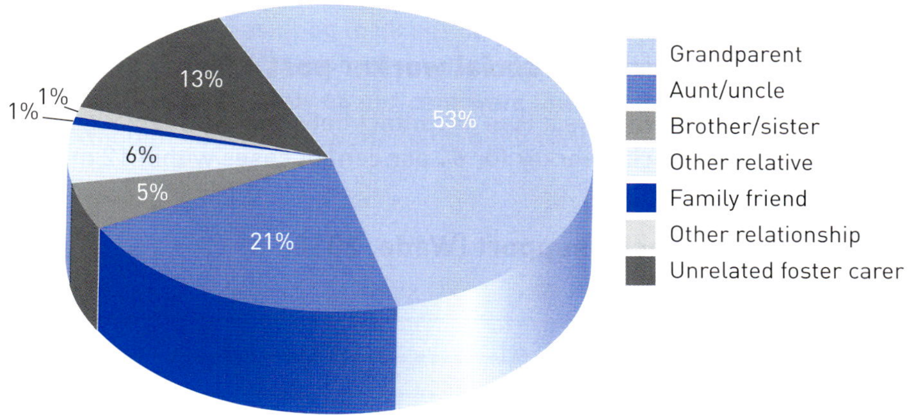

Type of placement prior to application

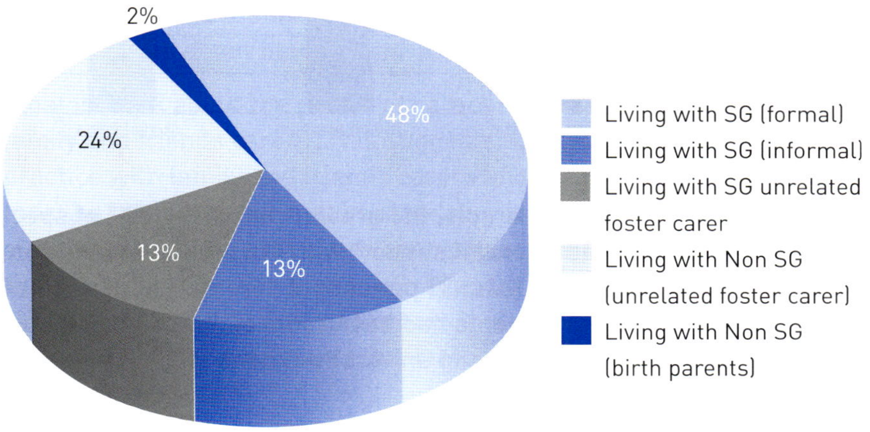

In the Hall sample, 24 per cent of the carers had not cared for the child before the order was made. Where the child was living with carers before the order, this was for less than two years unless they were local authority foster carers, where it was an average of 4.75 years. In the Wade study, 74 per cent of the children were already living with the carer. The average length of the pre-order placement was three years, but that ranged from three months to 11 years.

Contact

In the Hall sample, 60 per cent of birth parents had frequent direct contact with the child. All but three of these required contact supervision. Contact was supervised by the special guardian or by the local authority (at least in the short term). In the Wade sample, 88 per cent had face-to-face contact with their birth mothers, with monthly or

3

The role of the local authority in special guardianship

THE STATUTORY FRAMEWORK

A number of questions have arisen about the disparity between the comprehensive role of the local authority where a plan is for a child to be adopted or placed in foster care, and a local authority's "more limited" identified role in special guardianship. In particular, the question has arisen as to whether a local authority can *place* a child who is looked after for special guardianship.

The statutory framework identifies a specific set of functions for local authorities in relation to special guardianship, and this is described below. The fact that it is a private law application by a carer will not diminish the local authority's interest in the application or their duties and responsibilities towards the child. In many cases, notification by the carer to the local authority of their intention to apply for an order will be one step in a long series of steps that the local authority will have been a part of. In others, the notification and application will be in the course of public law proceedings with the possibility of competing plans for the child. All the lessons that have been learned about best practice in permanent family placement are likely to be relevant and therefore to be applied in special guardianship, irrespective of the private law status of the order or the pathway of the child and the applicants up to the application. That practice wisdom needs to be applied even though the regulations and statutory guidance are relatively silent when compared to that which is available in adoption and care planning. Above all, it is essential that any risks in this process are shared by the adults and not by the child. The disruptions, losses and upset that the child may have experienced already mean that any further disruptions, losses and upset must be avoided wherever this is foreseeable and possible.

The role of the local authority in relation to special guardianship can be summarised as follows:

- to ensure that special guardianship is considered and, where appropriate, planned for in respect of any child who is looked after;
- to investigate and prepare a report for court consistent with Regulation 21, SGR 2005/*Regulation 2, SG(W)R 2005* and the designated Schedule of each of those regulations;
- to provide a range of services, as set out in section 14F(a), Children Act 1989; Regulations 3, 4 and 5 of the SGR 2005 and *Regulation 3 of the SG(W)R 2005;*
- to provide financial support as set out in Regulations 6, 7, 8, 9, and 10 of the SGR 2005 and *Regulation 7 SG(W)R 2005* and periodically review that support as set out in Regulation 18 of the SGR 2005 and *Regulation 12 SG(W)R 2005;*
- to undertake assessments of support needs, as set out in Regulations 11, 12, and 13 of the SGR 2005 and *Regulations 6 and 7 SG(W)R 2005;*
- to provide notification of the outcome and decisions of those assessments, as set out in Regulations 15 and 16 of the SGR 2005 and *Regulation 8 SG(W)R 2005;*
- to deliver support services, as set out in Regulation 14 of the SGR 2005 and *Regulation 11 SG(W)R 2005* and monitor the outcome of that plan, as set out in Regulation 17 of the SGR 2005 and *Regulation 12 SG(W)R 2005.*

STRATEGIC AND OPERATIONAL MATTERS

Special guardianship is an important permanence option, although local authorities cannot directly make a placement for special guardianship or themselves make an application for a special guardianship order (there is no pre-placement order which is the equivalent of a placement order in adoption). However, through planning for permanence, they can make and enable a plan where special guardianship is the outcome. In order to deliver this, local authorities should have policies and procedures in place that incorporate their duties and responsibilities in respect of special guardianship. This should include the following core elements.

Strategy

Identifying where the strategic and operational lead is held for special guardianship in the authority. This will include how special guardianship is to be promoted:

i as a potential permanency option for children looked after where this is the right plan for them;

ii in contributing to the local authority's fulfilment of the "Sufficiency Duty" (England only).[3]

b Identifying the advantages and place of special guardianship in achieving permanence for children. This should include those children who are or become looked after, as well as those who are not looked after but where the local authority will be required to undertake assessments to prepare court reports following notification.

c Identifying how special guardianship support services are to be developed and made available compliant with Section 14F(a)(b), Children Act 1989, including how they might be integrated and developed alongside adoption support services, or any family and friends or fostering support services. This should include strategies for commissioning or arranging services delivered through other public bodies and private providers. It should also include how the authority will develop a strategy to enable a transparent and fair system for providing financial support consistent with the special guardianship regulations, statutory guidance and case law.

d Relevant aspects of this strategy should be identified in the authority's plan as required in section 4.2 of the *Family and Friends Statutory Guidance* 2011 (England only).[4]

Operational – care planning

e The quality assurance systems for planning for permanence where special guardianship is a potential outcome. Statutory reviews will need to consider which route to permanency is most appropriate for meeting the child's needs for secure and stable care. Independent Reviewing Officers will need to understand the relative merits and particular characteristics of special guardianship that achieve permanence for the child.

f Although there is no statutory role for panels in relation to special guardianship, as there is for adoption and foster care, the role of panels or other formal meetings to approve and quality assure any work in relation to special guardianship should be actively considered and implemented. Consideration should be given to the appropriateness of combining panel functions.

---

3 Section 22G of the Children Act 1989 and *Sufficiency: Statutory guidance on securing sufficient accommodation for looked after children* (DCSF, 2010)

4 http://www.education.gov.uk/publications/eOrderingDownload/Family%20and%20Friends%20Care.pdf

g The availability of information, skills and knowledge in social work teams working with family and friends and in fostering teams to advise, support and prepare both prospective special guardians and foster carers in relation to the relative merits of special guardianship and the permanent nature of this order. This should include transparent and agreed protocols for managing processes where the child is placed with foster carers who are registered with an independent fostering provider. This should include placement planning and the provision of support if a special guardianship order is made, as well as consideration of appropriate financial compensation for the loss of the carer to the provider.

h Information, advice, counselling and life story work with children to enable them to understand the nature of special guardianship and the plan that is being made. This must include specific work that enables them to express and have recorded their wishes and feelings about the plan and other matters in their history and circumstances that may be relevant to them now and in the future.

i Information for young people and their guardians about how they will be able to approach leaving care services to assess what advice and assistance might be offered to them if they are qualifying young people under sections 23 or 24 of the Children Act 1989.

j The availability of services to advise, counsel and prepare birth parents on the meaning and implications of special guardianship. Where appropriate, this should include access to independent advice and counselling.

Operational – reports to court

k There are no regulations that identify the minimum experience of social workers or the supervisory arrangements for assessing and preparing the report to court, as there are in adoption. Given the significance of the outcome for the child and the applicants, there is no reason to believe that principles set out in those regulations in relation to adoption[5] should not apply in relation to special guardianship, irrespective of whether the child is looked after or not.

l The systems that approve and quality assure reports to court. The care planning process for a looked after child will need to be co-ordinated with the advice and information, support and assessment of the prospective special guardian, so that the court is provided with sufficient evidence and analysis that demonstrates that the child's need for permanent secure care will be met by the making of the order.

5 www.legislation.gov.uk/uksi/2005/1711/contents/made

Particular attention will need to be paid to the location and availability of specialist advice to managers and practitioners.

m A system for allocating notifications from courts that an application has been made for a special guardianship order and a means of allocating that work.

n Arrangements, where appropriate, to commission independent social workers who are suitably qualified and experienced to investigate and write reports for court, section 14A(10), Children Act 1989. The supervision of such work should be addressed in those arrangements.

o The arrangements to work with other local authorities to supply relevant information in respect of a child or prospective special guardian where a report is being prepared.

p Proactive liaison with local courts to identify good practice and resolve matters of concern or difficulty in respect of special guardianship.

Operational – support

q The availability of quality assurance systems to ensure compliance with the assessment of need, planning, provision and review of special guardianship support.

r The availability of counselling, advice and information compliant with section 14F(a), Children Act 1989.

s The skills and knowledge of the workforce and services that enable the delivery of support compliant with section 14F(b), Children Act 1989 and Regulation 3, SGR 2005 and Regulation 3, SG(W)R 2005.

t Easy to understand and fair financial policies in relation to the remuneration of foster carers following the making of a special guardianship order, including appropriate equity for family and friends carers.

4

Applications for a special guardianship order

WHO CAN APPLY?

The legal framework for special guardianship established it as a private law order. The order can be made following application to a court by those who are eligible, following the submission of a report from the local authority covering both the suitability of the applicant/s to become special guardians, a full assessment of the needs and circumstances of the child and the identification of any support needs the child or prospective special guardian might have.

Section 14A(2) of the Children Act 1989 specifies that a special guardian must be 18 or over and cannot be a parent of the child. Sub-section (3) specifies that a court may make a special guardianship order on the application of an individual who is entitled to make such an application or has the leave of the court. There may be a joint application by more than one individual.

Prospective special guardians fall into one of five main groups.

1 Foster carers who have been approved by a local authority or an independent foster care provider and who are not related to the child.

2 Family and friends carers who have been approved as foster carers by the local authority.

3 Family and friends carers temporarily approved under Regulation 24 of the Care Planning, Placement and Case Review (England) Regulations 2010 and Schedule 4 and Regulation 38 of the Fostering Services (Wales) Regulations 2003.

4 Family and friends carers who are not currently caring for a child who is placed with either a local authority or independent foster care provider foster carer.

5 Others where the applicant and the child are unknown to the local authority until the notification to apply for an order is made.

resources and that works out well although not without cost. Before special guardianship was introduced, the most likely legal order to be used in family care cases was a residence order.

Where an application is made in respect of a child who is not looked after or known to the local authority, their pathway to a time established relationship can be equally as varied as for those children who are looked after. It is likely that, for many of these children, arrangements will have evolved within families resulting from an original temporary crisis in the parent's ability to care, to a situation that has become long term. For others, sudden tragic events may have required a more immediate long-term solution. The child's journey in any of these arrangements may have been a speedy transition into the current arrangement or it may have evolved over time with different carers playing a part until a more settled solution is found.

Consent – non-established relationships

The second group of people who are eligible to make an application are those where an agreement has been reached (including any necessary consents) that this is best for the child. This applies:

- where the child is in the care of a local authority and the local authority gives its consent to any person to make an application – ss14A(5)(c) and 10(5)(c)(ii) Children Act 1989;
- to any person who has the consent of all those with parental responsibility for the child – ss14A(5)(c) and 10(5)(c)(iii) Children Act 1989;
- to those who have obtained the consent of all those in whose favour a residence order is in force – ss14A(5)(c) and 10(5)(c)(1) Children Act 1989;
- to any person who has the leave of the court to apply – s14A(3)(b) Children Act 1989.

The special guardianship provisions extend to those where in any family proceedings concerning the welfare of a child, a court may make a special guardianship order if the court considers that an order should be made. This condition applies even where no application has been made and that may include consideration during any adoption proceedings.

These provisions indicate the flexibility of special guardianship to a wide range of circumstances. There are clear advantages to this, but there are also concerns that consent may in some circumstances indicate too little of the preparedness of prospective special guardians to undertake the significant responsibilities which the making of an order will confer. This may be particularly so where family and friends come forward or are identified in the course of care proceedings as potential carers. These issues are addressed more fully in Chapter 6, *Assessing prospective special guardians*.

5

Assessing the needs of children

FACTORS THAT NEED TO BE ADDRESSED

The schedule for the court report sets out those matters that need to be addressed in respect of the child. BAAF publishes a form that is compliant with these requirements. The facts that need to be presented to the court include the child's:

- family composition;
- social, cognitive, emotional and behavioural needs and development, including their wishes and feelings;
- educational needs and development;
- physical health needs and development;
- care history.

It is important that the child's history and needs are subject to appropriate analysis and evaluation and are presented in such a way that a clear evidence-based picture of the child is available to the court. The evidence and analysis should clearly lead to any recommendation as to whether or not a prospective special guardian can meet the needs of the child until they are 18. This analysis and evaluation should also form the basis for the assessment of special guardianship support.

The *Framework for the Assessment of Children in Need and their Families* (DH, 2000 and 2001 for Wales) and its associated materials set out a clear model for understanding and thinking about a child's developmental needs, the capacity of the prospective special guardian to meet those needs, and the wider social and environmental factors within which the family will function. The model takes an interactive perspective on these three domains and it sets the context for understanding the opportunities and the constraints for a child's development over time. The facts and information needed for the report give everybody involved an important opportunity to ask the question: 'Do and development across all domains – physical, emotional, behavioural and cognitive – and that this is available to the court. [6]

LIFE STORY WORK

Children need to have full and age-appropriate understanding of their history, circumstances, family and family membership both before they were born and afterwards (Ryan and Walker, 2007). Children differ in their curiosity and need to know but it is essential that all children have access to their life story and that this becomes a part of family history that is appropriately shared and celebrated. Life story work is an important part of this and needs to be considered and planned for in any special guardianship arrangement. It is important that the child is a full and active participant in constructing their life story through whatever means is helpful and meaningful to them. The significance of this can be seen in the quotation from *AJ* (Adoption Order or Special Guardianship Order) (2007) EWCA Civ 55. (2007) 1 FLR 507.

> *Asked whether he could tell his "Mom and Dad's" name he replied (with) his uncle's longstanding nickname and his aunt's first name. Asked whether he has another mother and father he replied without hesitation "Yes (his mother and father's first names)". He said he was living with his aunt and uncle because his parents couldn't look after him. They had been arrested, were naughty and shouted. He said he had not seen his parents do these things, but spontaneously added: 'But I'll go and get my red book (life story book). It's got the things they've done. I keep it under the stairs.' He then got the book, which contained various photographs and letters. The psychologist said it was clear that he knew where this was placed and appeared to have regular spontaneous access on demand.*
>
> (at 24)

SIBLINGS

In many notifications, it is likely that there may be more than one child. They may be full or half-siblings. It is important that there is an early understanding of the relationship between siblings, including paternity, through the construction of a family tree. There may be other siblings who are not a part of the prospective special guardianship family.

6 See BAAF forms IHA-C and IHA-YP

In planning the assessment, consideration must be given to how the history and characteristics of the sibling relationship are to be explored and what part they play and are likely to play in the future of the special guardianship family. Siblings should be seen together and separately and their respective wishes and feelings addressed in the report (Mullender, 1999; Argent, 2008; Lord and Borthwick, 2008; 2009).

IMMIGRATION STATUS AND UNACCOMPANIED ASYLUM-SEEKING CHILDREN

In any assessment or application for special guardianship, the immigration status of the child will need to be established. It will be important to establish what that status means in terms of the right to remain in the UK.

The statutory guidance for special guardianship identifies that it may be an appropriate order for some unaccompanied asylum-seeking young people. A stable and meaningful family life is as important for unaccompanied asylum-seeking children as it is for UK citizen children. The pathways to placement for unaccompanied asylum-seeking children may have some similarities to those for UK children. However, there are clearly other factors such as separation from their country and community of origin and likelihood of experience of war or other forms of conflict. The making of an order cannot fetter the discretion of the UK Borders Agency to exercise its powers, including removing the child from the UK.[7] A special guardianship order does not of itself allow the child to acquire citizenship or resolve outstanding issues in relation to immigration status.

Where the location of the child's parents and other family are unknown, the order has the advantage of not legally severing that relationship. If the information becomes available about their location or circumstances and contact is re-established, then the special guardian, the child and the birth parent will need to have detailed discussions about the implications of the new information. The power to apply to discharge or vary the order allows for unexpected developments in the circumstances of the child and the special guardians. But the assessment and report should not recommend the order unless there is a clear evidence base that both the prospective special guardian and the child are in a position to make a potentially lifelong commitment.

7 *R v SSHD ex parte T* (1995) 1 FLR 293; *Re A* (Care proceedings: Asylum Seekers (2003) 2 FLR 921; *Re L* (Care Order: Immigration powers to remove) (2007) EWHC 158(Fam)

c *the likely effect on him of any change in his circumstances;*

d *his age, sex, background and any characteristics of his which the court considers relevant;*

e *any harm which he has suffered or is at risk of suffering;*

f *how capable each of his parents, and any other person in relation to whom the court considers the question to be relevant, is of meeting his needs.*

Section 14A(8)(b) of the Children Act 1989 and Regulation 21 of the Special Guardianship Regulations set out the requirement for a report for the court and the Schedule in those Regulations sets out the matters to be dealt with in detail. The special guardianship guidance and case law make it clear that the report should be complete in all its sections. A proforma will be available from BAAF compliant with that Schedule.

PLANNING THE ASSESSMENT – ALLOWING TIME FOR FULL CONSIDERATION TO BE GIVEN TO THE PLAN FOR PERMANENCY

Planning for permanence in respect of special guardianship is different to that which drives other forms of placement. In *S (A Child)* [2007] EWCA Civ 54 (2007) 1FLR 507, the Court of Appeal states:

> *In most cases the issue will be not the actual placement of the child, but the form of order which should govern the future welfare of the child: in other words the status of the child within the household.* (at 48(iii))

The statutory framework for special guardianship does not envisage or allow a process of introductions, matching and supervised "settling in" in the way that is required in adoption. It does not allow for an interim period of reflection to assess how things are working out outside of the application to court and the preparation of the report. Instead, it assumes that the question of 'with whom the child should live' has more or less been settled because the arrangement has existed for legally specified periods of time or because the required parties have given their consent.

The assumption that children will already be living with the prospective special guardians, whether this is temporarily or fully approved by the local authority as a foster care placement or under some other arrangement, was core, although not exclusive, to the design of special guardianship. The fact that this may be so does not lessen the need for a full and comprehensive exploration of the issues in the report for court. But assessing something that has existed for some time and is thought to be working well is different to assessing something that is yet to happen, as is typically the case in approving foster carers or adopters before a child is placed. The task of planning and preparing the report where the notification has come from a time established relationship may be very different to planning and preparing the report where the child is not living with the carers or has only done so for a brief period. Additional pressure may come where special guardianship has arisen and is being considered in the course of care proceedings.

Practice experience supports the concern that special guardianship reports are being prepared without adequate time being available for reflection or for the relationship between the child and prospective special guardian to have become established. It is important that local authorities and others involved in long-term planning for children are clear that the combination of the need to avoid delay and the possibility that a special guardianship order may be made in the absence of opportunities to enable the important work of arranging, establishing, supervising and supporting the child and prospective special guardian does not lead to poor decision-making. There is long established good practice in planning for permanence through adoption and those principles should as far as possible be used when planning for permanence through special guardianship.

The expected period for the preparation of the court report is three months.[8] This may in many situations be sufficient, but in others the circumstances of the child and the applicant may make this too short a period of time for adequate advice, preparation and reflection, given the long-term implications of what is being planned for everybody involved. In those cases where notice of an application has been received and this three-month period is too short a period of time for the necessary pre-order work to be completed, the applicant could be advised to delay their application in order that sufficient preparation work can take place including, wherever possible, establishing and settling the child with the prospective special guardian. This issue is partially addressed in *Re S* (2007) where the court states that:

> *...in many cases, it may be appropriate to pause and give time for reflection, particularly in those cases where the order is being made of the court's own motion.* (para. 48 (iv))

Where an application to the court has been made and concerns exist about the adequacy of time for completing the report, then in the interests of the child and the applicant, the parties should identify and

---

8 The local authority must start their preparation of the report to court when they are notified of the intention to apply for a special guardianship order. Three months later the applicant can make their application. If at that stage the local authority needs more time to complete the report, they can make representations at the Directions hearing and explain why. There is an assumption that the report will be ready for the court at the time that the application is issued, but no duty imposed on the local authority to comply with that timescale, nor any sanctions for failing to complete the report within three months.

agree what necessary work needs to be done in order that a sustainable permanent placement can be evidenced. Submissions to and the agreement of the court will of course be a necessary part of any action needed to enable this.

It is important to acknowledge the structural and regulatory differences between special guardianship and adoption and foster care in respect of assessment and reports. When information, advice, training and preparation as well as assessment, review and agency decision-making are core to practice in adoption and foster care, there is every reason to believe that they are core to special guardianship best practice as well. It is a challenge to build them into a structure that envisages these matters are usually settled when they may well not be, under the pressures of a timescale of three months and a range of other issues that may also not be decided. The challenge of this is not underestimated. However, the task of planning and preparing the report to court should in every case be seen as an opportunity to comprehensively review and evaluate what has happened to date, what has been achieved so far, and what is anticipated in the future. It should be seen as an opportunity for the child (depending on their age and understanding), the prospective special guardian and the assessing social worker to reflect on what they have learnt from the past and in the present. This may include being asked to explore past experiences or current arrangements. Done well, the process should be experienced and looked back on as a positive achievement for all concerned.

ASSESSING FAMILY AND FRIENDS CARERS

It is a requirement of the Children Act 1989 that local authorities should always consider placing a child within the family before considering placement with non-related carers. In March 2010, 7,200 looked after children were cared for by family and friends carers in England[9] but this is a small proportion of the estimated 300,000 children who are cared for on a full-time basis by a family or friend carer. There are many good reasons why the placement of choice for many children is with family and friends carers. The strength of commitment, determination and sacrifice of related carers to the children they care for has been identified in two recent studies (Farmer and Moyers, 2008; Hunt *et al*, 2008). Family membership is very important to most people and the idea that children should be cared for by non-related carers, even for short periods of time, is unthinkable for most. The child may come to be separated from their birth parents but they are not separated from

9 Department for Education, Statistical First Release September 2010, Table A9

other family members whom they are likely to know and maybe know well. The pain of being separated from birth parents may be lessened by the experience of remaining within the family. The history of the child is likely to be known in detail by the carers and many aspects of their culture and ethnicity, religion, language and social class are likely to remain constant. Keeping in close contact with other family members is easier, including siblings and half-siblings who may be living elsewhere. Staying in contact with birth parents is also likely to be easier. Although the transition, separation and loss for the child must not be underestimated in whatever brought the placement about, family and friends care is likely to be the least disruptive of all permanence options for a child.

Evidence clearly indicates that the greater majority of special guardianship orders are being made to carers who are related to the child, with a significant majority of these being grandparents (Hall, 2008; Wade *et al*, 2010). This pattern will evolve as special guardianship matures but it is clearly very important that this evidence is recognised as local authorities develop their services for undertaking assessments and providing court reports. The assessment of family and friends carers is a specialist area and social workers undertaking such assessments need to be trained and supervised in the particular issues that can arise. The parenting capacity domain of the Assessment Framework is equally relevant in undertaking assessments where the child is being cared for by adults who are not their birth parents. The key issue is assessing the applicant's overall parenting capacity in understanding, responding to and meeting the needs of the particular child throughout their childhood (and beyond).

There may also be constraining issues with related carers and these will be particularly important when the objective of the placement is to secure a "family for life" for the child. Family and friends carers are not likely to have planned to care for the child even though they may have chosen and are motivated to do so. Doing so may have resulted from an emergency or a traumatic event. Where the carer is a grandparent, they may have had had other life plans which have then become disrupted and this may include retirement. Grandparents may also be approaching an age where ill health is more likely and there may be limits to their energy, resilience and longevity, although these must not be assumed without exploration and evidence. They may themselves be dealing with the consequences of their own child's disappearance, death, drug or alcohol abuse or serious mental health problems. This may have resulted in seriously strained relationships over a considerable period of time or a complete breakdown in these relationships. Some may be living in poor housing, on low levels of income and have access to low levels of support. None of this may result in them questioning their motivation and wish to care for the child, although the additional

a special guardian cannot change the child's surname[10] or remove the child from the United Kingdom for longer than three months without the written consent of every person with parental responsibility or the leave of the court. Lastly, special guardianship orders can be varied or discharged on application to a court. There are a number of specified parties that can make such an application:

- the special guardian themselves;
- any local authority in whose name a care order was in force with respect to the child before the special guardianship order was made;
- any person with a residence order in respect of the child before the special guardianship order was made.

The child's parents can apply for variation or discharge but only with the leave of the court and only if there has been a significant change in their circumstances since the special guardianship order was made.[11] Parents also have access to the courts for section 8 orders under the Children Act 1989, apart from seeking to apply for a residence order. A similar provision applies to any step-parent who has parental responsibility or any person who had parental responsibility immediately before the special guardianship order was made. The child may also apply with leave of the court if the court is satisfied that the child has sufficient understanding, but they do not have to show a significant change of circumstances.

The legal power to vary or discharge a special guardianship order is not intended to indicate that it is regarded as an interim or short-term plan. This is clarified in *Birmingham City Council v R* (2006) EWCA Civ 1748 (2007) 1 FLR 564.

> *In our judgment it is because special guardianship is an issue of very great importance to everyone concerned with it, not least, of course, the child who is its subject. It is plainly not something to be embarked upon lightly or capriciously, not least because the status it gives the special guardian effectively prevents the exercise of parental responsibility on the part of the child's natural parents, and terminates the parental authority given to a local authority under a care order (whether interim or final). In this respect, it is substantially different from a residence order which, whilst it also brings a previously subsisting care order in relation to the same child to an end, does not confer on any person who holds the order the exclusivity in the exercise of parental responsibility which accompanies a special guardianship order.*
>
> (at 78)

---

10 *Re L* (Special Guardianship: Surname) [2007] EWCA Civ 196; [2007] 2 FLR 50

11 *Re P* (Adoption: Leave Provision) (2007) EWCA Civ 616 (2007) 2 FLR; *Re G* (Special Guardianship Order) (2010) EWCA Civ 300, (2010) 2 FLR 696

An order applied for and granted indicates that the circumstances of the child are such that a solution needed to be found for them that establishes a permanent family life that is stable and secure and meets their needs. At the point of assessment and the court report, there should be clear evidence that the child both needs this and that this is what will happen if the order is made.

The making of the order will mean that the child will be living in a legally recognised family unit with all the expectations and advantages that this brings and inevitably, the stresses and challenges as well. It will be important that special guardians understand the significance of this and have openly thought about and discussed the implications and how they will manage this. Evidence should be collected and an assessment undertaken that a special guardianship order will create a strong boundary around the family and that the family will not be subject to uncertainty or anxiety caused by any other person trying to destabilise or change the family's sense of security by making unwarranted applications or seeking leave to make applications to vary or discharge the order. In particular, they will need to be in a position to establish a clear sense of authority in the family that allows them to regulate the boundary around the family. The prospective special guardian's capacity to do so needs to be explored sensitively and directly through the assessment process and in the court report. Addressing the issues during the assessment can make for a solid foundation for sensitively and openly finding a way to exercise authority to create a secure boundary as the family structure matures.

Establishing family boundaries and facilitating appropriate contact arrangements

All children have relationships with important people across the boundary of the family they live in – with those in their extended family as well as those whom they are not related to. These wider family relationships may be meaningful and significant for the child; they may just be routine visits that have little meaning; or sometimes they may be unsettling and unwelcome. It is for those with parental responsibility to ensure that these relationships are managed well and in the immediate and long-term best interests of the child. For children in special guardianship families, these extended family and friends relationships may have particular significance and pose particular challenges, especially where these relationships are with parents, siblings and others. A fundamental part of managing this well includes understanding the child's views and experiences of these relationships – their meaning and significance to the child. This can be difficult where the child continues to experience loss and longing and perhaps a hope for a new beginning and reconciliation with birth parents. It can also be difficult where the child is upset by these relationships and expresses a view that they do not want to have contact. These issues are further complicated when the placement is with family and friends and family history, loyalty and betrayal generate powerful emotional forces (Hunt *et al*, 2010).

Adoption practice has increasingly come to recognise that the primary feature that enables a child, the adoptive family and the birth family to adjust in a positive way to the experience of adoption is "communicative openness" (Neil and Howe, 2004; Brodzinsky, 2005). The development of this concept has identified that contact can too often be limited to specifying the frequency and type of contact and the practical support for this and not sufficiently on its purpose and meaning, particularly for the child. The concept of "communicative openness" recognises that all the parties in adoption need to be able to think about, discuss and be generally open to all the issues that adoption stirs up – the facts and circumstances that led to the adoption, the people involved, the meaning it has to those people and the differences between them and how that changes over time. This needs to become woven into the lived experience of all those involved. Special guardians and children also need to develop a "communicative openness" about what has happened to the child, the circumstances that brought the placement about, who the important people are in the child's history and story and what might happen in the future. Some of this may be painful and distressing. Putting thoughts and feelings into words about this and establishing a family culture where these can be expressed is most likely to benefit the child. The concept may need some modification in special guardianship placements, especially where they are with family and friends carers. In particular, the immediacy of family pressures in many situations may make openness particularly difficult. But the capacity of prospective special guardians to develop communicative openness in addressing these challenges and to be able to think about them and think them through should be an important part of the assessment.

Arrangements for direct and indirect contact as a part of communicative openness requires careful assessment, planning and justification, focusing on the immediate and the long-term needs of the child and the sensitivity, co-operation and resourcefulness of the special guardian, the parent/s and others. The assessment must address these issues. In its spirit of co-operative inquiry with all the parties, the assessment should establish as clearly as possible what the most likely and workable arrangements are, now and as far as possible into the future. Where there is a time established relationship, then this should build on what is already known to be working. Where the relationship is still to be established, then this will require a different kind of discussion.

Are other orders needed?

A court, in making a special guardianship order, may vary or discharge any other existing orders such as a contact order or a residence order made under section 8 of the Children Act 1989. The court must also consider whether a contact order should be made at the same time as the special guardianship order. There may be a delicate balance to be achieved in ensuring that the child's needs, the special guardian's needs and the parent's needs are met through the making of any other order or whether this is best left to the judgement of the special guardian, based on their knowledge of the child's needs. What must be remembered by all those who are a part of this process and contribute to achieving this balance is that the overriding need is to create a stable and secure family life for the child. It is only within that secure framework that these important issues can be addressed.

In a number of cases, special guardianship orders have simultaneously been made alongside supervision orders. Serious consideration should be given to the compatibility of the two orders being made alongside each other. In particular, it is important to ensure that there is no contradiction between the threshold conditions for making a supervision order, namely that a child 'is suffering or is likely to suffer significant harm' and that this 'is attributable to the care given to the child, or likely to be given to him if the order were not made' (S31(2), Children Act 1989), and the judgement that the prospective special guardian has sufficient authority and confidence to protect the child. If there is sufficient evidence to satisfy section 31(2), then it is essential to be clear that there is clarity and sufficiency of evidence to satisfy the making of a special guardianship order.

If there is evidence of destabilising parental interference in the special guardian family and uncertainty about the capacity of the special guardian to manage this effectively, then the source of the problem should be explored and solutions identified to address the problem. The problem may result from the prospective special guardian being unclear and needing support in establishing their parental authority in remaining focused on the child's needs when under pressure from parents or others. It may result from unpredictable, chaotic or threatening parents who have not accepted their child's need for an alternative family placement. In some instances, these problems may be resolvable through advice, information and counselling. They may also be resolvable through the provision of ongoing support, although this should aim to bring a resolution to the issues within a reasonable timescale. It is also important to bear in mind the possibility that the parent/s will use their right to apply to the courts for a section 8 order (apart from a residence order) and of the potential destabilising effect this may have on the placement. In some cases this may be resolvable through applying for a section 91(14) order which restricts this right unless the court gives leave. However, it should be noted that the test used by the court for the granting of leave in these circumstances is relatively low.

In a small number of cases, the issues may be assessed as so serious that urgent consideration should be given to whether special guardianship is the right order to secure the placement. It may be in some circumstances that an alternative legal order should be considered, such as adoption. If there are serious child protection concerns, it may be necessary to remove the child to a placement where they are sufficiently protected and where a new permanence plan can be identified and agreed.

Throughout the exploration of these difficult issues, there is a primary objective to assess the way in which the making of an order will enable the special guardian to establish a secure psycho-social boundary around the family and the child which enables their developmental needs to be met and enables a meaningful family life together. Other relationships must not unduly interfere with this primary objective. The challenges in establishing the evidence and the risks cannot be underestimated. Expert guidance and support may resolve some issues but the urgency of providing a stable, secure family life for the child must never be compromised by an over-optimistic belief that a resolution will be found in the course of time.

Identity and relationships

Special guardianship is a very significant transition in the life of a child – it marks a new beginning even though it continues relationships and a family life that have become well established. In another sense, it continues the story of the child's past and the way that they "arrived" in their new family. The child's identity will be fundamentally influenced by the fact that they are separated from their birth parent/s and have made a new identification with their special guardianship family. Whatever brought this separation about in the past will continue to have an influence over the present and the child's thoughts and feelings about this. This almost certainly will be a part of any contact arrangements with the child's birth parent/s. Even where a child has no contact, they are likely to be curious and to experience sadness and a deep sense of loss for their parents. How this has and becomes incorporated into the child's sense of who they are and what understanding they have of this is central to a good assessment.

The influence of the past on the present will be reflected in the names children use to refer to their special guardians. This may result from an explicit agreement between the child and special guardian or it may be what has arisen through "custom and practice" in the family. Sometimes this may be an accurate representation of the relationship – "Grandma" or "Grandpa" or "Aunt" or "Uncle" or the first name of the special guardian. Sometimes the term used may not be an accurate description of the relationship where, for instance, a child uses the term "Mummy" or "Daddy". There are no rules about what is right or wrong except that, whatever term is used, the child should have a clear, age-appropriate sense of their history, who their parents and other family members are and why they can no longer look after them. This should be the basis for life story work with the child and be incorporated into the way the family tells its history and establishes its culture. The stories told to support this should, wherever possible, be positive and realistically framed. At the same time, they should not avoid painful truths about the past, conveyed in child-appropriate ways.

The child and the special guardian will also need together to establish a "story" for the outside world to represent what has happened to create their new family. Special guardianship is a new concept and most people will still not be familiar with what it means. This will be significant where the family comes into contact with schools, general practitioners and other health professionals and other services which sustain ordinary family life. For the child, they will also need their own "story" to tell to friends or to use in school tasks where, for instance, they are asked to write personal accounts for school projects about their family or what they did in the holidays. While not every eventuality can be predicted, it is better for children to be as prepared as they can be to safely deal with these issues and not to be left surprised, confused or frightened when they come up.

Where the local authority has placed the child with approved foster carers who have then applied for a special guardianship order, consideration will have been given to the ways that the child's ethnicity, culture, religion and language will be addressed in placement. In placements with a relative, these issues can be more complex because the fact of "family membership" may be considered to outweigh those factors that are typically addressed in relation to ethnicity, culture, religion or language in "stranger" placements. But many children are born to parents who do not share similar backgrounds across one or all of these features. As an example, a child (boy) may therefore have a white Catholic mother from a Northern English town speaking English as her first language and a black, African, Christian father from Ghana whose first language is Akan. The special guardianship applicant is the maternal grandmother. There will be important questions to consider in the assessment about the attitudes and views of the grandmother towards the child's heritage and identity and her understanding of the importance of this to his development, even if there are no questions about the arrangements that are in place for him or with whom he should live. The assessment should address these issues positively and constructively, recognising their potential sensitivity. There may be issues identified that would benefit from the special guardian and the child receiving appropriate support.

The Schedule requires the local authority to take into account any expressed views that the child's birth parents have in respect of a child's religious or cultural upbringing and the willingness of the prospective special guardians to follow these wishes.

Birth parents and other family members

The Schedule requires basic factual information to be presented on the birth parents and other family members or other significant people the local authority considers relevant. It also requires the assessment to ascertain the wishes and feelings of the birth parents about the application and plan for special guardianship.

It is very important that the assessment identifies and plans for this work, given the significant consequences and impact the making of the order will have on the birth parents. It is essential that the birth parents have access to sufficient information and advice about special guardianship and counselling about the meaning that the plan has for them and their child. Because of the pathways to special guardianship, especially in time established relationships, they may have some, if not considerable, experience of the meaning of the placement and its implications for them. The existing status quo may therefore be disturbed by the application. However, it is important not to assume where this is so. An established and settled relationship does not mean that any one of the parties will not be stirred up to protest or express their unhappiness about what is being planned to happen. This does not mean in itself that the plan and application are not well justified but, as with many change processes, there may need to be some period of adjustment. Where the order is being considered in the course of care proceedings and in other situations as well, the issues may be controversial and indeed opposed. In any of these situations, the availability of independent advice, counselling and support may be particularly important.

Notwithstanding the fact that the making of the order does not terminate the basic legal link with the birth parents, it is important that a clear presentation is made of the restrictions that will be placed on the birth parents' ability to exercise parental responsibility and the legal options that are open to them if the order is made and is in force. It is important that they should be made aware of the plan for permanence for their child that lies at the heart of the application.

The Schedule requires that the parents' wishes and feelings are ascertained about the child's religious and cultural upbringing. The Schedule also requires that their wishes and feelings are ascertained in respect of contact with their child. It is clearly important that these wishes and feelings are fully understood and properly taken into account by the local authority and the prospective special guardians. However, they cannot have a determining effect on the plan of the local authority or the prospective special guardian unless a court determines that this should be so.

Special guardianship across borders

Where, in the notification of an application for a special guardianship order or during the assessment, it becomes clear that the plan is for the child to be taken out of the UK for more than three months, then the permission of the court will be required if the order is made. Managing special guardianship assessments in the best interests of the child across national borders is challenging. The duty to undertake the assessment and prepare the report to court and the provision of support as set in the regulations and guidance. However, the difficulties in resolving cross border issues are amply illustrated in *O v L, I and Orkney Island Council* [2009] EWHC 3173 (Fam) and can result in disputes that compromise the welfare and long-term planning for children.

Where the prospective special guardian is habitually resident[12] outside of England or Wales, a clear plan will need to be established about how to appropriately assess and prepare the report and its recommendations. This will include providing appropriate information and advice to the prospective special guardian, including the effect that the order will have in their own country throughout the child's minority and then into adulthood, including the entitlement or otherwise to citizenship. The assessment and provision of support, including practical and financial support, will also need to be taken into account, given the general circumstances in that country and the individual circumstances of the prospective special guardian. The wishes and feelings of the child and the likely impact on them of such a major change – the advantages and the challenges – will need to be fully addressed in the assessment.

The plan for the assessment will need to include appropriate arrangements for an assessment of the prospective special guardians to be undertaken in that jurisdiction. This will include seeking advice from specialists in undertaking such assessments such as Children and Families Across Borders.

12 'The place where the person had established, on a fixed basis, his permanent or habitual centre of interests, with all the relevant facts being taken into account for the purpose of determining such residence,' (*Marinos v Marinos* [2007] EWHC 2047 (Fam)).

OTHER REPORTS

References

The Schedule for the report (SGR, 2005, 4(v); *SG(W)R 2005, 4(n)* requires written reports to be prepared from interviews with the three persons nominated by the prospective special guardian to provide personal references. Guidance in local authority information to prospective special guardians should indicate that only one of these nominated referees should be a relative. Guidance on managing references is set out in the *Practice Guidance on Assessing and Preparing Prospective Adopters* (DfES, 2006, Chapter 2, pp. 12–25). Two sections are quoted below, suitably adapted.

> *Written references, followed by face-to-face interviews, should generally be sought by letter from three people, not more than one of whom should be a relative. In some cases it may be difficult to obtain satisfactory written references where there are language or literacy difficulties. If this is the case, the agency should record the reasons for not obtaining written references on the case record.* (Para. 12)

The letter from the *local authority* to the referee should ask for the following information and views:

> *in what capacity they know the prospective special guardian/s personally;*
>
> *how long they have known them and how often they see them;*
>
> *the prospective special guardian/s' child care experience, if any, and any related strengths and weaknesses;*
>
> *if the referee has children, how the prospective special guardian/s has interacted with and related to those children;*
>
> *how the prospective special guardian/s might cope with caring for and parenting a child;*
>
> *any concerns about the safety of a child placed in the prospective special guardian/s' home;*
>
> *if a couple are being assessed, the stability and permanence of their relationship; and*
>
> *any other information that the referee thinks may be helpful to the assessment.*
>
> (DfES, 2006, Para.14)

Health reports and summary

The Schedule for the report (SGR, 2005, 6; *SG(W)R 2005*) requires that a summary is prepared by the medical professional who provided the information in respect of:

- (1(l)(*2(d) for Wales*) a health history and a description of the state of the child's health which shall include any treatment the child is receiving. The significance of the transition for the child and the applicants should mean that the assessment should be the same format as that used in pre-adoption health assessments.[13]
- (4(k))(*4(h) for Wales*) a health history of the prospective special guardian including details of any serious physical or mental illness, any hereditary disease or disorder or disability. The significance of the transition for the child and the applicants should mean that the assessment should be in the same format as that used in pre-adoption health assessments.[14]

Enhanced Criminal Records Bureau (CRB) checks

A local authority is not required under the Special Guardianship Regulations to undertake enhanced CRB checks on prospective special guardians or other adult members of their household. However, the Home Office states:

> *The responsibilities of special guardians involved means that it can be considered as working within a "Regulated Activity" under the Safeguarding Vulnerable Groups Act, making it eligible for an Enhanced CRB check.*
>
> (Home Office, 2010; see also DfES, 2006, Chapter 2, paragraphs 6–9)

Other checks

The Practice Guidance on assessing and preparing prospective adopters (DfES, 2006, Chapter 2) makes recommendations about other relevant checks. These may be important in respect of prospective special guardians but the local authority will need to exercise its discretion depending on the circumstances of the individual application and the information it already holds.

- Former partners – paragraphs 21–25
- Local authority reports – paragraphs 26–28
- Employers – paragraphs 30–32
- Children's schools – paragraph 33
- The probation service – paragraph 33

---

13 See BAAF Form IHA-C/IHA-YP

14 See BAAF Form IHA-C/IHA-YP

and what is yet to be accomplished. This will be set out in the report to court and can be done with confidence given what can be evidenced from what has happened before.

The transition to special guardianship for children in settled local authority placements will begin with the local authority clearly setting out its plan about the assessed support needs once an order is made. This includes the provision of financial support and what services it expects will be made available or existing services it plans to terminate. This will reflect the local authority's strategic and operational objectives in respect of special guardianship and its understanding of the needs of the child. This will need to be explained and explored in detail with the prospective special guardians and be subject to any further assessment of need that the prospective guardian may request or that the local authority undertakes.

Children not in time established relationships

For some children, the local authority may only be in the early stages of getting to know the child's needs and there may be little that is settled or which is evidence-based. Where the child has only been living with the prospective special guardian for a relatively short period of time, and for some children this may include those situations where the child is not living with the prospective special guardian, there will be particular challenges. These situations will require a different approach in identifying the immediate and longer-term support needs of the child. This does not lessen the need for there to be a comprehensive and evidence-based assessment of those needs, but the confidence with which those needs are identified and particularly the effectiveness of any services may be significantly less than for children in time established relationships. Being realistic about the "unknown" and the "untested" should be reflected in the court report.

THE SUPPORT NEEDS OF CHILDREN IN SPECIAL GUARDIANSHIP FAMILIES

Caring and supportive relationships – attachment

A central part of family life is relationships, one core component of which is an attachment relationship. A child who has had a poor start in life, especially where they have been abused and/or neglected and experienced significant separation and loss, may have developed patterns of attachment that are insecure or disorganised. This can be confusing and distressing to the carer when the child's need for proximity to and sensitive and appropriate responsiveness from the carer is expressed through behaviour which is difficult to understand or is overtly rejecting or hostile. Carers can be left feeling confused, angry or rejected in such circumstances and these can create spiralling patterns of difficulty. The consequences of such patterns can result in the child being without access to emotionally sensitive and supportive adult care that appropriately calms and reassures them when they are anxious or distressed. The long-term consequences for the child and the carer of such negative patterns can be serious (Prior and Glaser, 2006; Schofield and Beek, 2006).

Social, emotional and behavioural difficulties

The origin and development of this complex range of issues may be rooted in early experience and, in particular, attachment, separation, loss and instability. The issues may also have their origin in genetic factors or exposure to toxins such as alcohol, nicotine and/or illegal or legal substances during pregnancy. Other causative factors may be physical or emotional trauma resulting from the combined impact of various forms of maltreatment, neglect and poor parenting.

The impact of these difficulties on the child can be experienced both inside the family, in school and in friendships. The absence of difficulties in one area does not mean that this will be so in others. School may be a positive environment and experience for the child but they may express their anxiety and upset at home with the special guardian/s. Each assessment needs to be comprehensive to establish as far as is possible the possible causes of any difficulty and effective, evidence-based approaches to addressing them.

Services that understand and can support and work with the child and the special guardian where there are identified social, emotional and behavioural difficulties are very important. Close working arrangements with Child and Adolescent Mental Health Services (CAMHS) that are sensitive to the needs of families formed through special guardianship are crucial in enabling this. A range of evidence-based interventions and behaviour management programmes (e.g. KEEP (www.keep.fostering.org), Webster Stratton (www.incredibleyears.com), Fostering Changes (Bachmann *et al*, 2011), NICE (http://guidance.nice.org.uk/PH28/Guidance/pdf/English) are available and should be utilised wherever possible.

Education and school

For many special guardianship families, education and school will be a positive experience for the child that promotes learning and development and a sense of achievement and progress. It will usually be the source of friendship for the child and give access to a wide range of recreational transition for all young people and something that is usually celebrated and appropriately marked. For most young people, the transition to adulthood is built on a secure base that was established from birth, maintained through inter-dependence on parental figures and other family members, and increasingly incorporates independence as competence and maturity develop. Inter-dependence on parental figures and others continues as independence becomes more firmly established, but for most young people that stretches well into their 20s.

Special guardians will be faced with many of the same issues that any family faces when their adolescent children make this transition, with questions such as 'Who am I?', 'Who am I to become?' and other questions including those of ethnic and sexual identity. There are likely to be particular issues through this period arising from the decision-making that led to the making of the special guardianship order, including the place of parents in the future life of the young adult.

A prospective special guardian should have been encouraged to think about these issues at the point of application and during their assessment. Every special guardian will need to have thought about and developed a view about the post-18 transition issues. It is to be expected that, post-18, the young person will continue their family life with their special guardians and this will include all of the usual family activities and supports that any young person naturally associates with family membership.

Special guardianship will inevitably bring its own particular challenges for the young person and the special guardian as they navigate early adulthood. For some, particular difficulties will arise for which support may be necessary. The local authority does not have a duty to undertake an assessment for support needs post-18 unless the young person is an eligible child under leaving care regulations. In many circumstances, accessing universal services through education, health or community-based young people's services will be appropriate and providing information and advice on the availability of these will be sufficient. For others, more specialist support may be required and assessments will need to be undertaken through gateway services such as general practitioners, higher and further education, housing and the benefit system.

Access to leaving care services

A young person subject to a special guardianship order may be eligible for advice and assistance under the Children (Leaving Care) Act 2000 where they were looked after before the order was made. In order to qualify for such advice and assistance, there are certain age restrictions which apply.

- The young person must be 16 but no older than 21.
- Where the young person is under 18, the order must still be in force.
- Where they are over 18 and under 21, the order must have been in force when they reached 18.

The local authority that has responsibility to provide advice and assistance is the one that last had responsibility for the child when they were looked after. However, there may be many circumstances where the delivery of advice and assistance may be more appropriate in the local authority area where the young person actually lives with their family. The National Protocol concerning inert authority arrangements for care leavers may be helpful where responsible authorities may wish to seek the assistance of area authorities in offering support to young people in these circumstances. Where special guardianship orders are made, the responsible authority will need to ensure that information about the young person, who may in future "qualify for advice and assistance", is retained so that it can be accessed by leaving care services.

Entitlement to advice and assistance is set out in the Children Act 1989 section 24(1A) and is described in section 24A. The local authority has to assess the young person's needs to establish that the young person needs help of a kind that can be given under section 24A or 24B and that the person who was looking after him 'does not have the necessary facilities for advising or befriending him'.

Following this assessment, the local authority may advise and befriend the young person (s 24A(3)). They may also give assistance (s24A(4)). Assistance may be given in exceptional circumstances as accommodation or cash (s 24A(5)). The local authority may also give assistance under section 24B, which allows the authority to contribute towards expenses of education and training, and costs of living near their place of education, training or employment, or to provide accommodation in vacations. Any assistance is subject to section 17(7)–(9), which allows it to be conditional on repayment and can take the means of the parents into account.

The availability of assistance for university fees, accommodation and other forms of support is a matter of discretion and so is subject to the policies of individual local authorities.

Variations and discharges

Special guardianship is one of a range of options that provides permanence for children who cannot live with their birth parents. In planning for permanence through special guardianship, it should be clearly evidenced that the order is the best available option for the child and provides a secure, stable and long-lasting family life.

8

Assessment, the plan, outcomes and effectiveness in special guardianship support

ELIGIBILITY FOR AN ASSESSMENT

There is a distinction in the special guardianship regulations between those situations where a local authority *must* undertake an assessment for special guardianship support and those where it *may* undertake an assessment. Where a child is looked after or was looked after immediately prior to the making of an order, the local authority *must* undertake an assessment upon the request of the child, the special guardian or prospective special guardian or parent. In any other circumstances, the local authority *may* undertake an assessment. The request for an assessment may come from a child, a special guardian or prospective special guardian, a parent, a child of the special guardian or any other person whom the local authority considers has a significant and ongoing relationship with the child.

Who is eligible for an assessment?

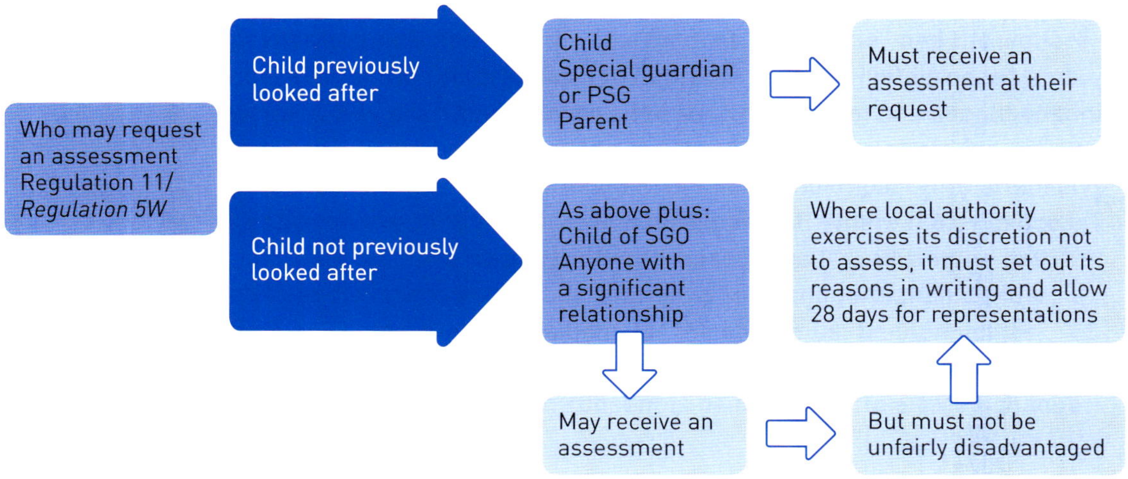

It is important that information is available to those who may be eligible and considering a request for an assessment of their support needs. This should include points of contact for requesting an assessment and the process for the assessment. This information should be available in appropriate community languages and in formats suitable for users with special communication needs. It should also be available in a format that is appropriate for children and young people.

The distinction between those where local authorities *must* undertake an assessment and those where they *may* is an important one. However, the English statutory guidance makes it clear (para. 51) that this distinction should be subject to a "fair" process as there will be examples where the pathway taken by the child into their current care arrangement is a matter of chance in terms of whether they ever became looked after or not. It is also important to note important court decisions defining those local authority actions that are considered to amount to a child being looked after whatever the local authority's own interpretation of its actions (see *London Borough of Southwark v D* [2007] EWCA Civ 182 and *R (on the application of SA) v KCC* [2010] 2FCR 405).[16]

Where discretion is exercised and a decision is made not to undertake an assessment, the local authority must give notice to the applicant of their proposed decision in writing, setting out the reasons for that decision. The local authority's application of the "fairness" principle must form a significant part of the explanation. The local authority should also consider offering alternative sources of assessment and support from universal services or the voluntary sector.

The schedule for the report to court requires that, where a local authority has decided not to provide support services, the reasons for this are explained in the report. A similar approach should be taken which deals with both the issue of eligibility, the application of the "fairness" principle and the advice that has been given to those subject to the assessment of alternative sources of support.

16 Subject to appeal

The assessment for special guardian support

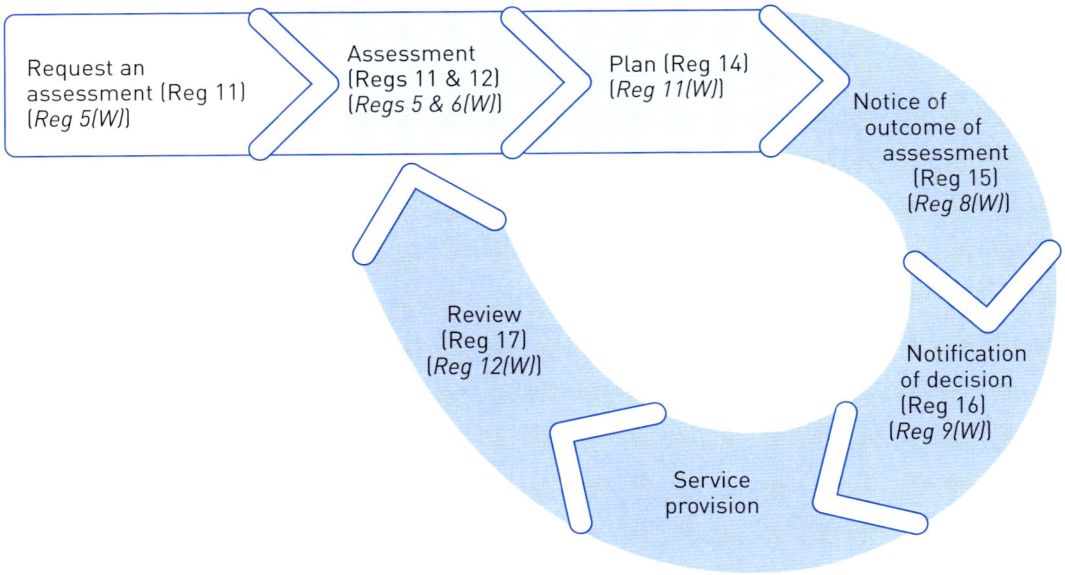

The process for undertaking an assessment is set out in the SGR 11–13 and *SG(W)R 5 and 6* and is detailed and specific about the steps that need to be followed. These steps are set out to ensure that the process is evidence-based, balanced, fair and transparent. It is important that support assessments build on what is already known about the child and their carers. In the assessment undertaken for court prior to any order being made, there will often be an established support plan where the child is in a settled and approved local authority placement. The discussions and planning up to the notification will provide a strong evidence base about how that will be a base for the development of a special guardianship support package.

For notifications where the local authority has little or no previous involvement with the applicant, there will need to be a fuller assessment that will determine the needs of the child and the applicant for the court report and whether this will become subject to an agreed support package while the application is heard and/or following the making of any order.

THE PROVISION OF SUPPORT SERVICES THAT MAY NOT REQUIRE AN ASSESSMENT UNDER REGULATION 12

The English statutory guidance states that an assessment is not always necessary in order to provide information, advice and counselling services (para. 55). The provision of information, advice and counselling is an essential part of the preparation for any family placement. The significance of the plan and decisions and their lifelong consequences must mean that no prospective special guardian, child or parent embarks on the process without being made aware and having the opportunity to think through the implications of what is being proposed. This should not be optional and not subject to a pre-assessment of need. Ensuring that the time and resources necessary to undertake this work are available to meet this objective is essential.

Special guardianship regulation 11(4) */Reg 4(3SG(W)R* sets out that, where it is clear to the local authority that a request relates to the provision of a particular service, or that that service is what is required, then the assessment can be specific to that service. One example might be a request for support in relation to contact. It may be very clear that the issue is specific and that mediation needs to take place between the parent and special guardian and that a more comprehensive assessment is not relevant.

Where the local authority is proposing to undertake other assessments in order to discharge its duties towards the child, special guardian or other relevant party, section 14F(10) of the Children Act 1989 gives it the power to carry out the assessment for special guardianship support services at the same time. This might include assessments carried out in relation to care planning, adoption support assessments on other children in the household and assessments for special educational needs.

Special Guardianship Regulation 19 (England only) allows local authorities to take urgent action to provide services where otherwise the regulations require them to follow the procedure as set out in Regulations 12–17. The welfare and safety of the child and stability and security of the placement should always be the primary consideration in determining service provision and this is recognised in this regulation. Where urgent action has been taken, it will always be important to follow up the service provided to assess the situation that led to the emergency, how these might be predicted or avoided in the future, and whether what was provided proved to be effective.

THE PROCEDURE TO BE FOLLOWED IN THE ASSESSMENT

Regulation 12 */Reg 6 SG(W)R* sets out the procedure for undertaking an assessment of special guardianship support services. It is important that those undertaking an assessment understand the purpose of assessments as well as following the required procedure. Assessments should ensure that the needs of the person requesting the assessment are properly evaluated and understood based on established evidence from child and family development, and enable all those affected by the issues as far as possible to come to a common and shared agreement about those issues and what should happen next. Assessments should be based on established facts or objective evidence and informed by the *Framework for the Assessment of Children in Need and their Families* (Miller and Bentovim, 2007).

Regulation 12(2) /*Reg 6(1)(b)SG(W)R* sets out the importance of interviewing those who requested the assessment, the child and any other person who may be significant to the issues being explored. A good assessment should leave all those subject to the assessment feeling that they have learned something about themselves and the situation being assessed. In order for this to happen, assessments need to be undertaken with sensitivity, empathy and insight and proceed on the basis of partnership and the avoidance of blame.

An assessment should be proportionate to the situation under assessment. An initial evaluation will need to be made of the seriousness and complexity of the presenting problem in order to establish an appropriate assessment format. Where this involves consulting with external agencies such as CAMHS, schools or other services, this will need to be agreed by the local authority with those agencies or services and an appropriate timescale for response established with them (Regulation 12(3); *Reg 6(1)(c) SG(W)R).*

An assessment should also include an evaluation of risk and an assessment of the effectiveness of the service against cost. Not all needs can be met even though they are identified needs. This will inevitably result in some frustration and disappointment, and this must be acknowledged and sensitively dealt with. Transparency and fairness are key to this.

Some identified needs do not have readymade solutions to them. Where a child has had a poor start in life, they may struggle to "catch up" and may show the consequences of developmental delay and/or trauma for many years. Some issues do not lend themselves to solutions where there is a conflict of interest as there may be in contact disputes or in a parent's continuing disagreement to the basis of the placement or the order. Assessments may capture much of this and be able to describe it and the potential consequences but not turn the clock back and start again. Again, transparency, openness and fairness established through the spirit of partnership are likely to be the most constructive approach to these difficult issues.

Stage 1 Assessment

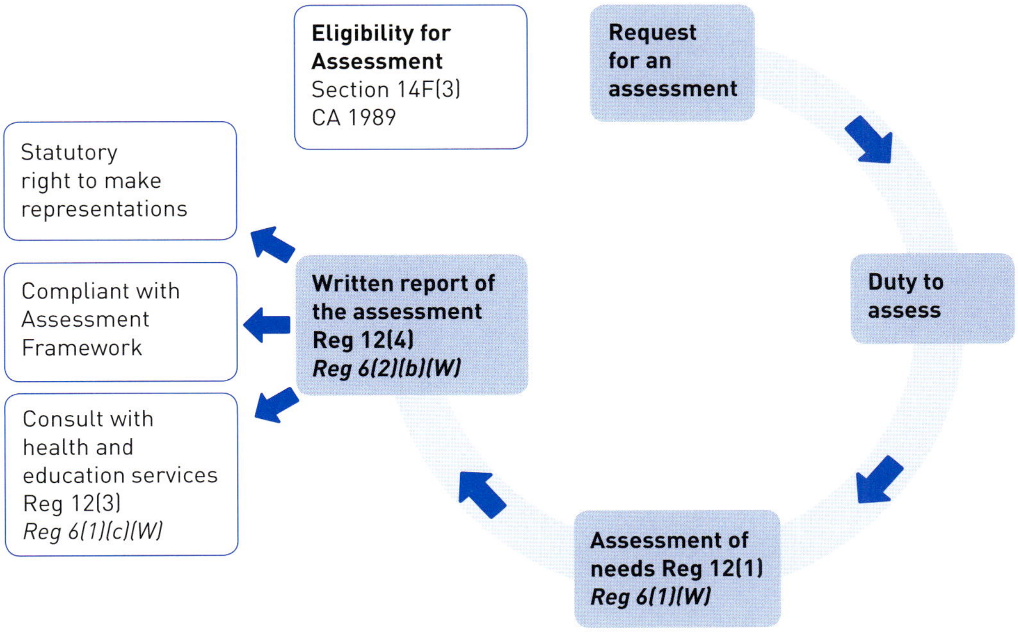

THE WRITTEN REPORT FOLLOWING THE ASSESSMENT

Regulation 12(4) /*Reg 6(2)(b) SG(W)R* requires that, following an assessment, the local authority prepares a written report. This report will be the basis for any subsequent local authority action, and the basis for a statutory notice of the proposed decision under Reg 15(2) /*Reg 11(4) SG(W)R*. This notice must include:

- a statement identifying any relevant needs in relation to special guardianship support;
- when the assessment is focused on the need for financial support, the basis and process by which this has been determined;
- whether the local authority is proposing to provide the applicant with support services and what those services are to be; where it is proposing to provide services; a draft plan for those services (see below);
- if financial support is to be paid, the amount proposed to be paid and any conditions to accompany that payment.

In addition to the statutory notice, the local authority should provide the applicant with contact details for relevant sources of independent advice and advocacy. It must also allow the applicant to make representation about the accuracy of the assessment, the basis upon which the notification has been constructed and any other comments which might be relevant. The notification must allow a reasonable time period for the applicant to make their representations and it is suggested that this is normally 28 days.

Where the applicant is a child, it is essential that the notification is written or accompanied by an explanation that reflects the child's age and level of understanding. It is also important that the notice be made available to an adult whom the child trusts who can explain the notice and discuss it with the child. This is likely to be the prospective or existing special guardian or another advocate who knows the child well. In some cases, this may require an independent advocate for the child.

The proposed plan

Regulation 14 /*Reg 11 SG(W)R* requires that a draft plan must be prepared when the local authority proposes to provide support services. Where the plan proposes to provide services which are the responsibility of health or education services, the local authority must consult with those services before it prepares the plan. Where other service providers are proposed to deliver services, then they must be consulted as well. Clarity of purpose is essential for the delivery of effective services and inter-agency co-operation is key to this.

The plan is intended to ensure that the proposed service(s) relate to the needs as identified in the assessment. As such, the objectives for the proposed service should be identified, the criteria by which the success or otherwise of the service is measured should be identified and the timescales for this. While this is the basis for sound and effective professional practice in any area, it should not be underestimated how challenging this process can be. Some programmes of intervention have become manualised and there is a strong evidence basis for their effectiveness. Parenting training programmes such as KEEP, Webster Stratton and Fostering Changes are good examples. There are other interventions and forms of help that are not evidence-based although they are thoroughly embedded in practice.

In order to ensure that the outcomes from services in relation to need are reviewed, a named person must be identified to monitor the plan (Reg. 14(4) England only). It is important that this person is able to take an objective perspective on the plan and its proposed and emerging effectiveness in order to properly discharge this responsibility. It is also important that they are familiar with appropriate ways of monitoring and evaluating effectiveness consistent with the complexity of the task.

Representations

The local authority must allow any person who has been subject to an assessment to make representations to them. In order to do this, it must give appropriate notice to that person, which sets out under Regulation 15(3) */Reg 8(2)(c)(d) SG(W)R*:

a a statement of the person's needs for support services;

b where this is in relation to financial support, the basis on which this has been calculated;

c whether there is a proposal to provide support;

d the services (if any) that are proposed;

e if financial support is being proposed, the amount payable;

f any proposed conditions for financial support as set out in Regulation 10(2) */Reg 8(2)(d)(ii) Wales*.

Where the proposal is to provide services and the local authority is required to prepare a plan, then a draft of that plan must be supplied with the notification.

The local authority's decision

Stage 2 Planning and decision making

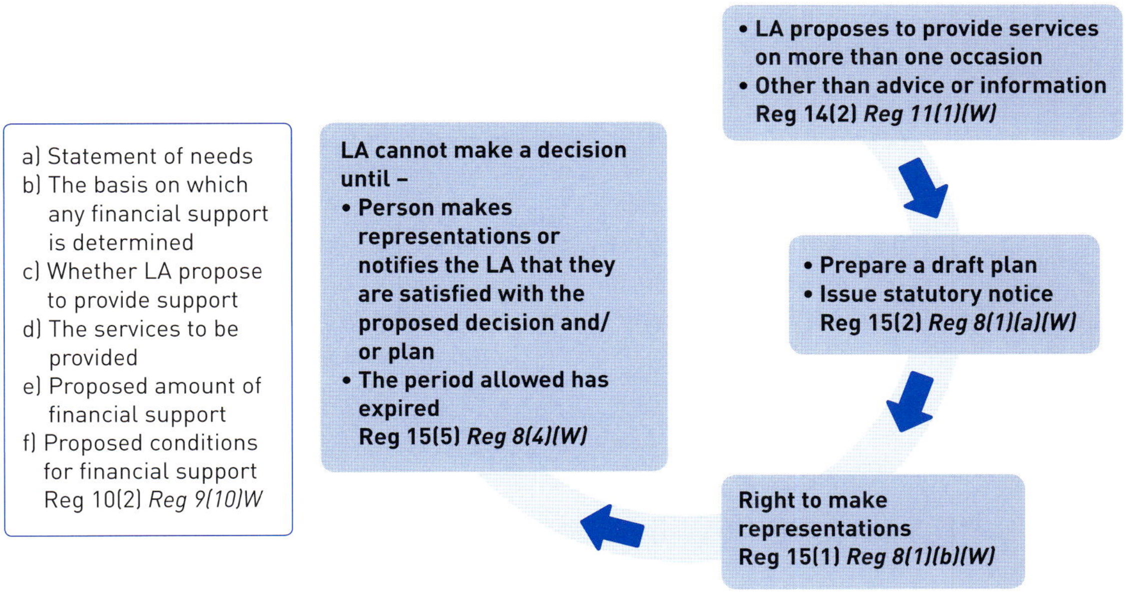

The local authority cannot make a final decision about support until the person assessed has made representations or notified the local authority that they are satisfied with the proposed decision and/or the draft support plan. If the period for representations has expired, the local authority can also then make its decision.

Before making its decision, the local authority will want to take into account any representations made. It should consider any new information provided in representations and the degree to which this influences its understanding of the needs of the child, the special guardian or other people who have been part of the assessment. It will also need to consider that information in relation to the local resource context informed by any statutory duties and responsibilities that apply, the strategy and policy of the local authority, any relevant case law and the principles of transparency and fairness. The overall driver in any decision must be the safety and welfare of the child and their need to establish a secure and lifelong family base.

NOTIFICATION OF THE DECISION TO PROVIDE SPECIAL GUARDIANSHIP SUPPORT SERVICES

When the local authority has made its decision, it must issue a notice of that decision under Regulation 16(1) */Reg 9(2)(Wales)* to the individual who has been assessed. The decision must be explained in that notification. Where the local authority has taken a decision to supply support services, it must provide the plan that sets out in detail what those services are and who will monitor the plan under Regulation 14 / *Regulation 12 (Wales)*.

It must be anticipated that not all requests for assessments will result in the provision of services identified by the person being assessed. The notification and explanation may therefore be a source of disappointment and frustration in some cases. But if the assessment has been done well and in a spirit of openness and transparency, recognising that there are often different perspectives and ways of understanding situations and particularly resource constraints, then even if disappointment and frustration are real, a person should be left feeling that they have been treated with respect.

MONITORING AND REVIEW OF SUPPORT PLANS

The importance of identifying the objectives of any service provision, and monitoring and reviewing the effectiveness of these services in meeting needs has already been discussed. The points which trigger a review are identified as a change in the circumstances of the person in receipt of services, at a point in the delivery of services that is considered appropriate or at a minimum annually. Reviewing a service or intervention throughout its delivery allows everybody involved an opportunity to learn and think through the benefits and disappointments of the service provided. The assessed needs may have been met completely by the service, partially or not at all. Different people may have different perspectives on this. The child's perspective will be particularly important in this, and reviews should ensure that they have an opportunity to contribute wherever possible. Where things have gone well, this should be recognised and appropriate recognition given. Where things have not gone so well, no blame should be attached but the opportunity used to identify why and what might be learned as a result. This may result in the local authority proposing to terminate the service or vary it to take into account what has been learned or achieved along the way.

The local authority is required under Regulation 17(4)(England) / *Regulation 12(5)(Wales)* to give the person in receipt of the service an opportunity to make representations by issuing a notice of the proposed decision and the time allowed to make those representations. The notice must set out the information that will already have been supplied under Regulation 15(3) /*Regulation 8(2)(c)(d)(Wales)* suitably modified. Where there is a proposal to revise an existing plan, the person must be supplied with a draft of that plan.

As in the original stages of the decision-making process, the local authority is required to take any representations made within the specified timescale. It can then make a decision to vary or terminate the service and revise the plan. Again, as with the earlier stages of the process, it must supply the person with a notice of that decision and a detailed copy of the new plan.

Stage 3 Review

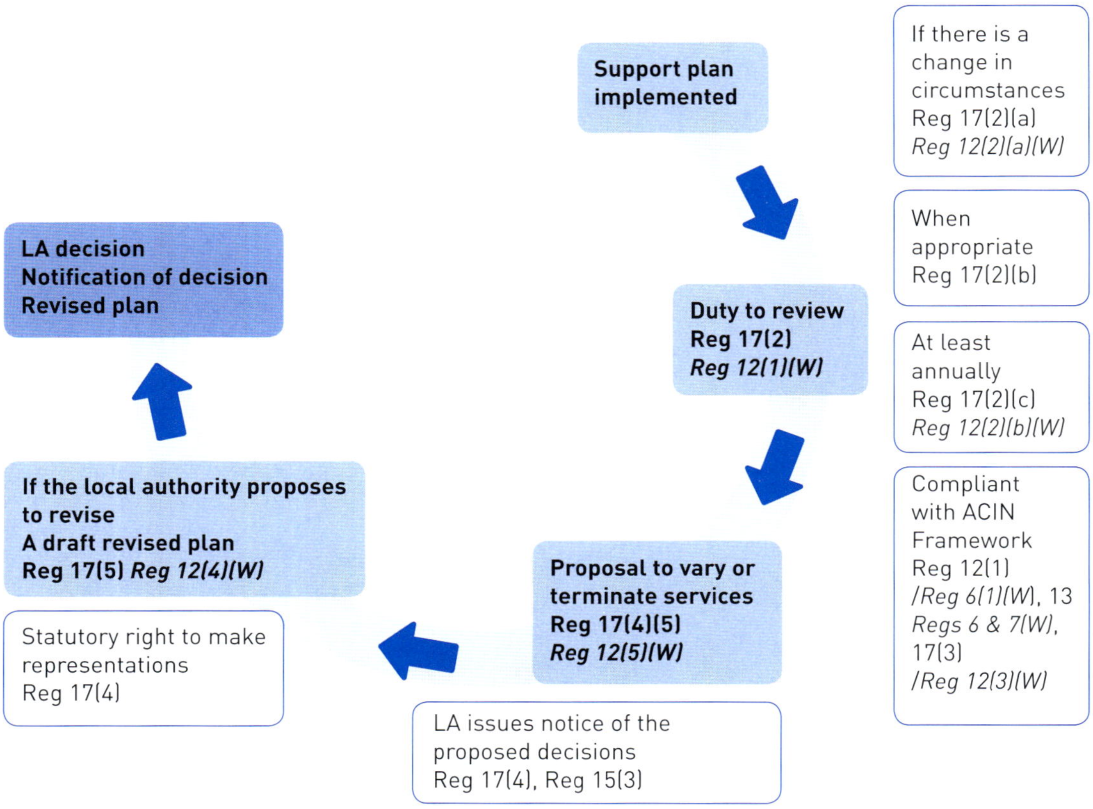

The regulatory framework for identifying needs, identifying a plan and agreeing that plan is demanding. Monitoring, evaluating and reviewing that plan are equally demanding. But there are important principles underlying these regulations about good practice. Engaging with service users, including children, discussing their views, experiences, thoughts and feelings, reaching a common understanding and identifying differences of perspective are essential to providing effective practice. The regulatory framework supports that process but its proper and effective implementation requires professional knowledge and skills and resources. Implemented without these, the framework could become a troublesome bureaucratic exercise and, at worst, a battleground that results in the breakdown of relationships with all the risks that entails for the welfare of children.

FINANCIAL SUPPORT

The provision of financial support is an important part of the special guardianship framework and the process already discussed in the preceding section about assessment, planning, provision, monitoring and review applies to financial support. This covers both the general provision of financial support and the specific issue of remuneration to former foster carers.

The statutory guidance indicates that 'financial issues should not be the sole reason for a special guardianship arrangement failing to survive' (SGG, para 37 /*SG(W)G, para 67*). It also indicates that, as a central principle, the regulatory framework enables local authorities to provide financial support to secure a special guardianship placement where it otherwise could not be made (Reg 6 and SGG para 37 *Reg 4SG(W)R and SG(W)G, para 67*). These are wide-ranging powers and reflect the importance special guardianship has in enabling children to live in a secure family environment. The duty to assess for financial support makes a distinction between children who are or were formerly looked after, but the guiding principles in the guidance are that the advantages of a permanent placement so outweigh the disadvantages of other pathways for the child that this distinction should always be driven by the principle of the child's long-term needs and welfare.

It is important in assessing prospective special guardians that the holistic assessment of parenting capacity across all its dimensions is the primary focus. While financial support must not be the sole reason for a placement not going ahead, it is also important that it does not become the primary issue in deciding that it should. Adoption assessments take into consideration the applicant's access to financial and other practical resources. No prospective adopter can be ruled out on the grounds of inadequate income but the assessment will explore this issue in detail and the general expectation is that prospective adopters will have established a means of securing a level of income that is sufficient for their needs, together with an absence of unmanageable debt. Similar considerations will apply to housing. The requirement to assess and establish stability and security in prospective adopters clearly must take finance, housing and other practical considerations into account. Struggling with debt or the stress of other financial issues will not adequately allow special guardians to focus on a child's needs and welfare.

The general expectation in special guardianship was that the child would be in a settled placement and that financial security and housing issues and other practical matters would have been addressed throughout that pre-order period. Where the child is looked after, the local authority will have been involved in establishing this as a part of their responsibility towards the child in placing them with foster carers. The primary issue in these types of placements will therefore be the transition from those arrangements that have applied while the placement was a foster care placement to those anticipated if the order is made. In order to effect this transition, there will need to be detailed assessments and planning to enable a secure financial package to be agreed between the parties.

The greater difficulty will be those children who are not in settled placements although the child is looked after, and where there are questions about establishing a placement for them including the financial support that they may need. There will be others where the local authority is not looking after the child even though there may be safeguarding or welfare concerns. Local authorities have the discretion not to assess in these circumstances but they also have a responsibility not to allow a special guardianship arrangement to fail due to lack of financial or other practical support. This can pose particular difficulties in family and friends arrangements where relatives have stepped in at short notice and subsequently make an application for special guardianship. Their circumstances may be such that they are in a precarious position where their income and other practical resources are only sufficient to meet their own needs. They do, however, have the commitment and determination to provide a home for the child but lack the means to do so. While the primary responsibility must be with universal state benefits to provide in such circumstances, the local authority has its own powers and duties on a case-by-case basis to secure such placements when it considers that it is in the best interests of the child to do so. Each local authority should ensure that its policies and strategic framework[17] clearly indicate how this will happen, with clear guidance and procedures to managers and practitioners responsible for individual cases. The budget for such provision should be clearly identified in each local authority's strategic plan.

The provisions of Regulation 6 *Regulation 4SG(W)R* are set out below.

17 Statutory Guidance on Family and Friends Care 2011, England.

Financial support: when is it payable?

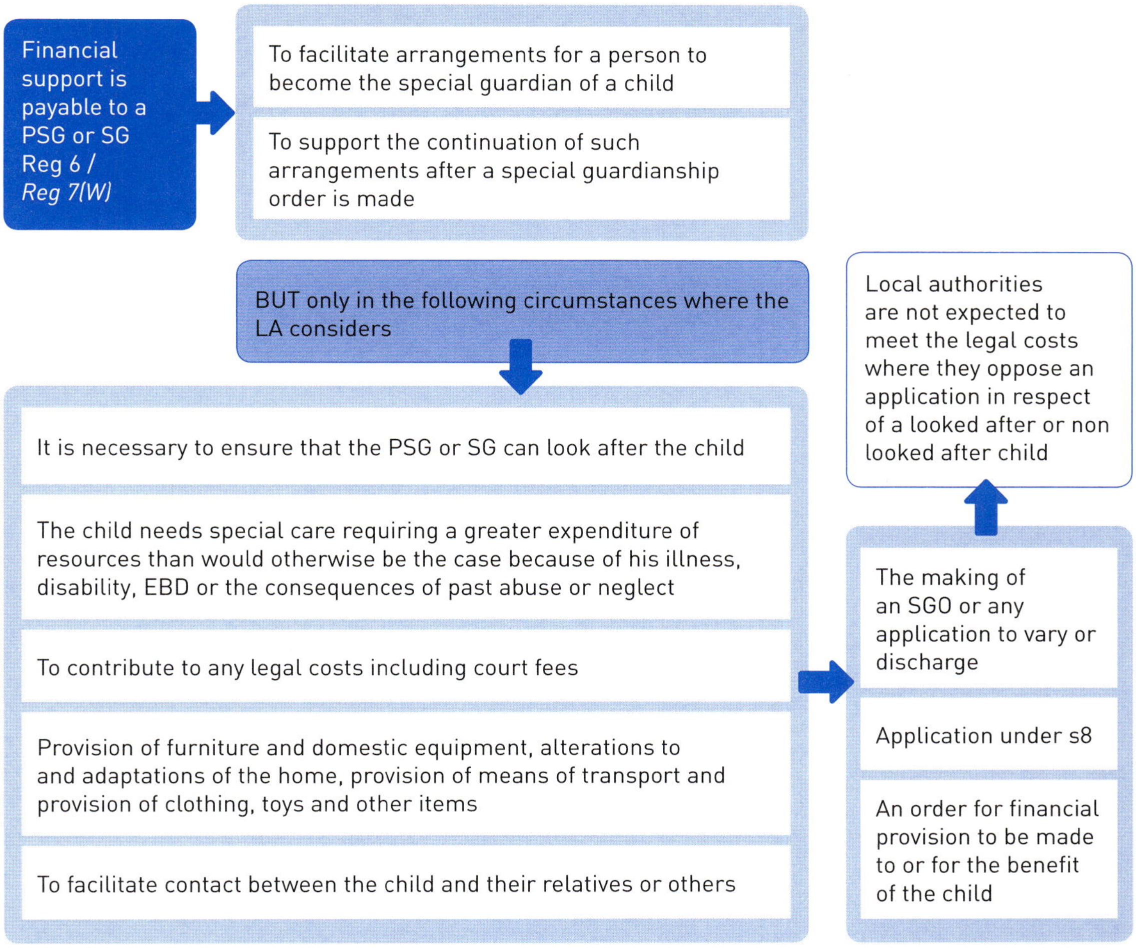

The focus of the regulation is clearly on the needs of the child and supporting the special guardian in meeting these needs. While there is a general responsibility to ensure the material circumstances of the placement are sufficient, there are more specific responsibilities to ensure that children who have special needs, whether resulting from past maltreatment or not, are properly addressed. There are also specific requirements in relation to contact in recognition of the ongoing and often complex nature of these arrangements.

ASSESSING FOR FINANCIAL SUPPORT

The provision of financial support must always begin with ensuring that prospective special guardians or special guardians fully access all available benefits and tax credits to which they are entitled. The support regulations do not allow local authorities to duplicate any payment which is available from other sources and, in assessing for support, the calculation must include any grants, benefits, allowances or resources available to the prospective special guardian or guardian. Regulation 13 */Regulation 7 (Wales)* sets out the matters that the local authority must consider in assessing for financial support.

Local authority calculation of financial support

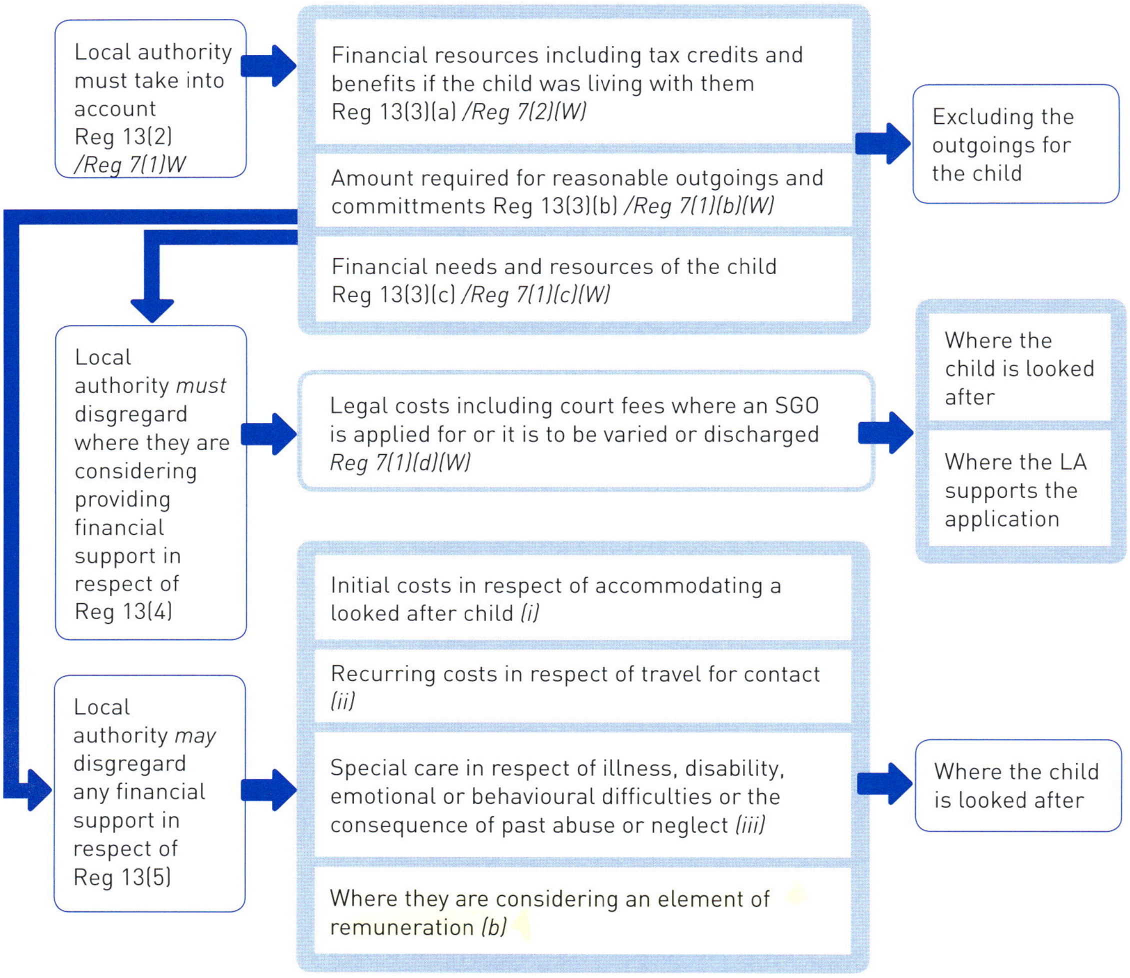

Remuneration for former foster carers

In establishing its baseline for calculating support and determining the amount payable, the local authority should use its fostering allowance scheme. This should reflect whatever the core allowance is plus whatever enhancements are payable in respect of the child, given their needs. This baseline should then be used as the maximum payment the local authority uses for that individual assessment and any means test used should relate to that maximum payment. The same baseline should be used for both related and non-related carers. The Department for Education has made available a model means test for use by local authorities in discharging this responsibility.[18]

The making of a special guardianship order indicates a profound shift in the circumstances and responsibilities of a local authority or independent provider foster carer. The making of an order will move the special guardian, if they are a foster carer, from the public sphere, where they will have combined their personal commitment to care for children with formal recognition and approval from an agency, including payment for their services, to the private sphere where the rewards for caring for a child are personal in the same way that they are in ordinary family life. Regulation 7 (England) /*Reg 7 SG(W)R* allows local authorities to continue to pay the remuneration element previously paid to a former foster carer to support the transition post-order. This may continue for two years from the date of the order and, if the needs of the child or other circumstances are exceptional, for longer.

The calculation of the remuneration element to former foster carers is set out in the statutory guidance (para 65). This states that the calculation 'should have regard to the amount of fostering allowance which would have been payable if the child were fostered'. This has been disputed. In *B v London Borough of Lewisham* [2008] EWHC 738 (Admin) 2008, Lewisham argued that the similarity between the special guardianship guidance and the adoption support guidance allowed them to calculate the amount based on their adoption allowance scheme. Mrs Justice Black notes at 46:

> *...it would, in my view, be unlikely that those responsible for the guidance intended that local authorities would go through the motions of reminding themselves of their fostering rates only to abandon them completely in all their subsequent considerations and to fasten instead on a quite different and much more stringent financial regime.*

The judgement continues at 54:

> *Whilst I accept that the guidance does not have statutory force, the local authority had a duty substantially to follow it unless there was good reason to do differently. Nothing that they have argued in these proceedings comes close to justifying a radical departure. It would appear that in reality they have failed to understand the central importance that paragraph 65 gives to the amount paid by way of fostering allowances and they cannot therefore have had regard to those allowances in the way in which they were required by that paragraph to do. They made, instead, a rigid link with adoption allowances which was not in accordance with the guidance. It follows that their resulting scheme is unlawful.*

18 www.education.gov.uk/childrenandyoungpeople/families/adoption/a0065904/adoption-practice-guidance-and-tools

The reference to fostering allowances is not contained in the Welsh guidance. However, the judge's later comments go beyond the regulations and guidance and consider the general lawfulness of paying an allowance for one type of placement which is significantly less than another.

The judge concludes at 57:

> *...a local authority is not free, in my view, to devise a scheme which fails to do what is required by regulation 6 or which dictates that some types of placement for a child carry a significant financial disadvantage in comparison with others or, worse, would impose such a financial strain on a carer that they would be forced to choose another type of placement. This local authority's scheme does this in relation to the grandmother and for that reason and in the light of the local authority's failure to have proper regard to the regulations and guidance is unlawful and must be quashed.*

In *Barrett v Kirklees Metropolitan Council* [2010] EWHC 467 (Admin) (12 March 2010), the local authority were subject to a review of their calculation of the special guardianship allowance in relation to their fostering allowance. In conclusion, HH Judge Langan at 29 says:

> *Kirklees' decision of March 2006, and the policy enunciated in February 2007, to pay SGOA at two-thirds of core fostering allowance, involved a substantial departure from the relevant ministerial guidance. No sufficient justification for that departure has been provided. It follows that the decision and policy were, and the policy remains, unlawful.*

Remuneration to former foster carers

The purpose of the two year transitional provision is to enable local authorities to maintain payments to foster carers who become special guardians, at the same rate as they received when they were fostering the child. This should give the family time to adjust to their new circumstances.

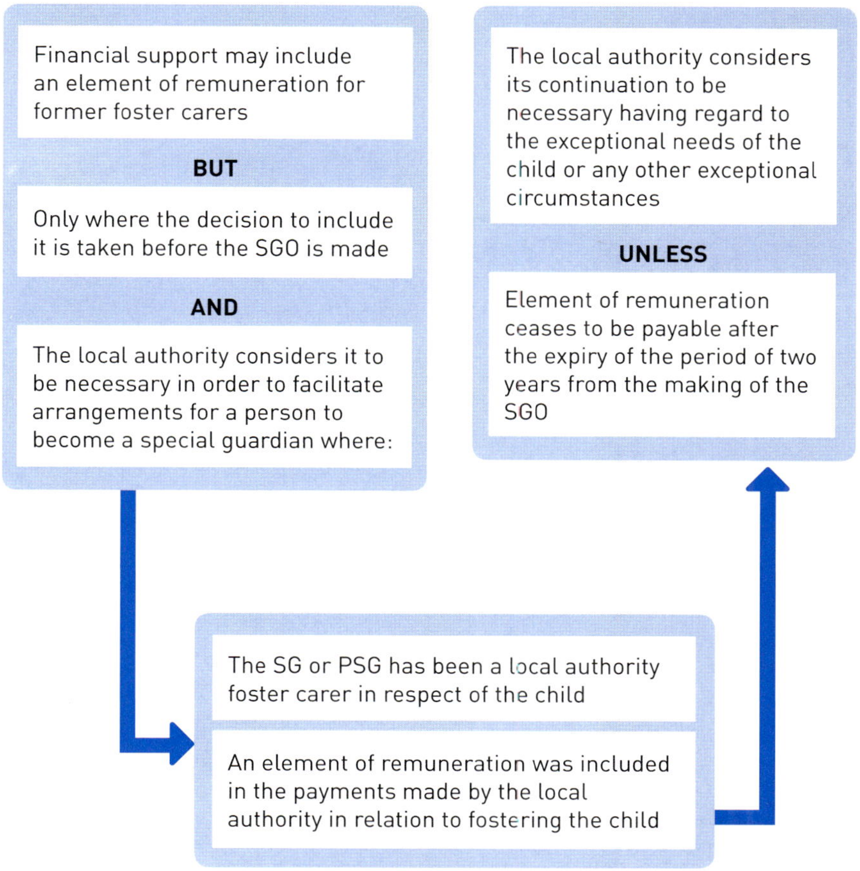

Notice of the outcome of an assessment for financial support

The procedure required following an assessment of need for special guardianship support also applies to assessments for financial support. Regulation 15 /*Reg 6 SG(W)R 2005* sets this out and this is discussed above. In addition to other requirements, the post-assessment notice must include the basis upon which the financial support has been determined and, if financial support is to be paid, the proposed amount. The time for representations must be stated and any representations taken into account where the local authority proposes to provide support.

Notice in respect of financial support

Where the local authority plans to provide financial support, Regulation 16 /*Regulation 10 (Wales)* requires that it issue a statutory notice which includes the following information.

Notification of decision Reg 16(3) /*Reg 9(5)(6)(W)*

The LA must give notice Reg 16(2) *Reg 9 (2)(W)* The notice must address:

- The method used to determine the amount of financial support
- Whether it is to be paid in installments or periodically
- The amount
- The frequency
- The period for which it is to be paid
- When payment will commence
- Where it is a single payment, when it will be paid
- Any conditions and consequences imposed by Reg 10(2) /*Reg 9(10)(W)*
- Procedure for review, variation and termination
- The LA's responsibility to review under Reg 17, Reg 18 /*Reg 12(W)*
- The responsibilities of the PSG or SG in any agreement under Reg 10 /*Reg 9(W)*

LA must review where payments are periodic in accordance with Reg 18 /*Reg 12(W)*

Conditions of financial support paid periodically

Regulation 10 /*Reg 12(W)* specifies that, where a local authority is proposing to pay financial support periodically, then it cannot do so until the prospective special guardian or special guardian agrees in writing to the following conditions.

Conditions

PSG or SG agrees that they will inform the local authority immediately if – (agreement in writing must be submitted within 7 days of any verbal agreement)

Reg 10 /*Reg 12(W)*

1 They change their address

2 The child dies

3 There is a change in financial circumstances or needs or resources of the child which may affect the amount of financial support

4 Any changes specified in Regulation 9

Reg 9 /*Reg 12(W)*

1 The child ceases to have their home with the PSG or SG

2 The child ceases full-time education/training and enters employment

3 The child qualifies for income support or jobseekers allowance

4 The child reaches 18 (except where they continue in full-time education/training where it may continue until the end of the course/training)

Review of financial support paid periodically

Where a local authority provides financial support and this is payable over specified periods, it must review that provision.

Review

Where the local authority provides periodic financial support, it must be reviewed (Reg 18 / *Reg 12(2)(W)*)

1 On receipt of the annual statement from the special guardian (Reg 10 /*Reg 12(2)(b)(W)*)

2 If there is any change or breach in the circumstances of the special guardian as specified in Reg 10 /*Reg 12(2)(a)(W)*

3 At any stage in the implementation of the plan where the local authority considers this to be appropriate

SUPPORT SERVICES FOR PERSONS OUTSIDE THE AREA

In England, Regulation 5 specifies the responsibilities of a local authority in providing support services when the person lives outside of their area. Those relevant are:

- a child who falls within the special guardianship regulations where they are looked after or were looked after immediately prior to the making of an order (Reg.5(1)(a));
- a special guardian or prospective special guardian of a relevant child;
- a child of a special guardian or prospective special guardian of a relevant child.

This responsibility expires three years from the date of the order unless it involves the provision of financial support and the decision to do so was made prior to the making of the order (Reg. 5(2)).

This regulation does not prevent a local authority from providing support to a person who lives outside of their area when they have assessed it as appropriate to do so.

In Wales, *Regulation 3(2) SG(W)R 2005* does not prevent the provision of special guardianship support services to a person outside the local authority's area, in accordance with the regulations.

USEFUL RESOURCES

A comprehensive list of useful organisations for family and friends Carers is set out in Annex D of the *Family and Friends Care: Statutory Guidance for Local Authorities* 2011 (England only)

LEGISLATION

Children Act 1989

Adoption and Children Act 2002

The Special Guardianship Regulations 2005 (England)

The Special Guardianship (Wales) Regulations 2005

Special Guardianship Guidance 2005 (England)

Adoption and Children Act 2002 – guidance to support the Special Guardianship (Wales) Regulations 2005.

Family and Friends Care: Statutory Guidance for Local Authorities (England) 2011

REFERENCES

Argent H (2008) *Ten Top Tips for Placing Siblings*, London: BAAF

Argent H and Coleman J (2006) *Dealing with Disruption*, London: BAAF

Bachmann K, Blackeby K, Bengo C, Slack K, Woolgar M, Lawson H and Scott S (2011) *Fostering Changes*, London: BAAF

Biehal N, Ellison S, Baker C and Sinclair I (2010) *Belonging and Permanence: Outcomes in long-term foster care and adoption*, London: BAAF

Broad B and Skinner A (2005) *Relative Benefits: Placing children in kinship care*, London: BAAF

Brodzinsky D (2005) 'Reconceptulizing openess in adoption: implication for theory, research and practice', in Brodzinsky D (ed) *Psychological Issues in Adoption*, Westport, CT: Praeger

Department for Children, Schools and Families (2010) *Sufficiency: Statutory guidance on securing sufficient accommodation for looked after children*, London: Stationery Office

Department for Education and Skills (2006) *Preparing and Assessing Prospective Adopters*, London: DfES Publications

Department of Health (2000) *Framework for the Assessment of Children in Need and their Families: Practice guide*, London: Stationery Office

Farmer E and Moyers S (2008) *Kinship Care: Fostering effective family and friends placements*, London: Jessica Kingsley

Fursland E (2010) *Social Networking and Contact: How social workers can help adoptive families,* London: BAAF

Fursland E (2011a) *Foster Care and Social Networking: A guide for social workers and foster carers*, London: BAAF

Fursland E (2011b) *Social Networking and You*, London: BAAF

Hall A (2008) 'Special guardianship and permanency planning: unforeseen consequences and missed opportunities', *Child and Family Law Quartley*, 20:3, pp 359–77

Home Office (2010) CRB News November 2010, accessed at www.crb.homeoffice.gov.uk/resource_library/crb_news/crb_news_nov_10.aspx.

Hunt J (2009) 'Family and friends care', in Schofield G and Simmonds J (eds) *The Child Placement Handbook*, London: BAAF

Hunt J, Waterhouse S, and Lutman E (2008) *Keeping them in the Family: Outcomes for children placed in kinship care through care proceedings*, London: BAAF

Hunt J, Waterhouse S and Lutman E (2010) 'Parental contact for children placed in kinship care through care proceedings', *Child and Family Law Quartley*, 22:1, pp. 71–92

Lane M and Shah S (2007) *Special Guardianship: What it is and what it means*, London: BAAF

Lord J and Borthwick S (2008) *Together or Apart: Assessing siblings for permanent placement*, London: BAAF

Lord J and Borthwick S (2009) 'Planning and placement for sibling groups', in Schofield G and Simmonds J (eds) *The Child Placement Handbook*, London: BAAF

Miller LB and Bentovim A (2007) *Assessing the Support Needs of Adopted Children and their Families*, Abingdon: Routledge

Mullender, A. (1999) *We are family: Sibling relationships in placement and beyond*, London: BAAF

Neil EC and Howe D (2004) *Contact in Adoption and Permanent Foster Care: Research, theory and practice*, London: BAAF

Performance and Innovation Unit (2000) *Prime Minister's Review of Adoption*, London: Cabinet Office

Prior V and Glaser D (2006) *Understanding Attachment and Attachment Disorders: Theory, evidence and practice*, London and Philadelphia: Jessica Kingsley Publishers

Ryan T and Walker R (2007) *Life Story Work*, London: BAAF

Schofield G (2003) *Part of the Family: Pathways through foster care*, London: BAAF

Schofield G and Beek M (2006) *Attachment Handbook for Foster Care and Adoption*, London: BAAF

Schofield G and Beek M (2008) *Achieving Permanence in Foster Care*, London: BAAF

Sinclair I (2007) *The Pursuit of Permanence: A study of the English child care system*, London: Jessica Kingsley Publishers

Talbot C and Calder M (2006) *Assessment in Kinship Care*, Lyme Regis: Russell House

Wade J, Dixon J and Richards A (2010) *Special Guardianship in Practice*, London: BAAF